Conversations With Top Real Estate Investors Vol. 5

With contributing Authors

Bob Synder

Michael Andrews

Amy & BirdDog Berteaux

Wanda I. Carrasquillo

Michele L. Carson

Scott Fredricey

John & Karen Gill

Jeff & Janet Grenier

Scott & Allison Huminsky

Candie Baker De Jong

Jill Nettesheim

Steve Nordfors

Scott O'Shaughnessy

Derrick & Paula Porter

Jessyka Scala

Riley Shock

Glen Suerte

Adam Sullivan

Brian Visconti

Joshua White

Woody Woodward

D.U. Publishing
www.dupublishing.com

Warning—Disclaimer

The purpose of this book is to educate and inspire. This book is not intended to give advice or make promises or guarantees that anyone following the ideas, tips, suggestions, techniques or strategies will have the same results as the people listed throughout the stories contained herein. The author, publisher and distributor(s) shall have neither liability nor responsibility to anyone with respect to any loss or damage caused, or alleged to be caused, directly or indirectly by the information contained in this book.

ISBN: 9780998234090

Table of Contents

Introduction

Have you ever wanted to be sitting at the table when major real estate transactions were happening just to be able to glean insider information? If your answer was, "Yes" then this book is dedicated to you. You are going to be like a fly on the wall as top real estate investors are being interviewed and sharing their tips and strategies to being successful. These are honest and raw interviews with the intent to inspire you to follow your real estate dreams.

Bob Synder

Renatus was founded and is led by 25-year entrepreneur, Mr. Bob Snyder. As CEO and President, Mr. Snyder is responsible for day-to-day company operations, affiliate marketing program expansion, course curriculum evaluation and renewal, practitioner-instructor recruiting, and month-over-month increased sales performance. Mr. Snyder began his entrepreneurial journey over 25 years ago with the desire to leave a positive mark on the world. Establishing himself as a marketing leader, he gained first-hand knowledge of what drives marketing and team-building success. Mr. Snyder built and managed sales organizations with tens of thousands of individuals, achieved top status in multiple companies, and became a top income earner in the direct selling industry. He has freely shared his formula for success as he served on more than a dozen leadership counsels and advisory boards in the direct sales industry, received recognition in national publications as an expert in his field and has personally mentored over a dozen marketers to become seven figure earners. After years of building and growing marketing teams, Mr. Snyder's vision transitioned him into developing companies to expand the entrepreneurial spirit that has made this country the world's economic leader. He has founded and co-founded dozens of companies that have collectively produced hundreds of millions of dollars in revenue. His real estate company completed over 2,500 real estate transactions while his former education company trained over 60,000 entrepreneurs on the subject of real estate investing and business ownership.

Contact Info: www.MyRenatus.com

Shannon:

According to Forbes magazine, real estate is one of the top three ways that people become wealthy. As a real estate expert, why do you feel that this is the case?

Bob:

Because real estate is one of the three basic human needs: food, water, and shelter. There's always going to be a demand for real estate. Tech companies come and go, financial companies come and go, media companies come and go, but real estate is constant, and we are always going to have a need for it. Those individuals who position themselves with the right kind of properties are always going to be able to generate monthly cash flow.

Shannon:

Is that what inspired you to get into real estate: supply and demand?

Bob:

No. What inspired me to get into real estate was my wife. She dragged me kicking and screaming into real estate.

Here's the thing, I didn't understand it, and we always fear what we don't understand. I had been raised with the idea that a secure retirement required investments in the stock market. The problem was that I kept giving money to my broker and I continued to GET broker!

My wife was increasingly frustrated that we kept losing money on Wall Street, even from our conservative mutual fund investments. They weren't producing any kind of a sustainable return. By contrast, her mother and father invested in real estate while she was growing up. They made a habit of buying properties, paying them off, selling them, and buying others to build their portfolios. They developed cash flows that would take care of them in their retirement. Today, my father-in-law is eighty-eight years old and he and his wife live very comfortably from their paid-for real estate. The proof's in the pudding.

So, after losing a bunch of money on Wall Street my wife came to me and said, "Listen. We need to be in real estate. It's the way to build and secure our future and our kids' future. It's not Wall Street. It's not the stock market and it's not this other nonsense that you've been dealing with." Unfortunately, I was stubborn. I did not want to listen to her, but she was right and the last thing in the world I ever wanted was to tell her that she was right.

Shannon:
Now, looking back, you think, "Thank Goodness she was right."

Bob:
Yes, and think about what happened as a result of that, but it didn't happen overnight. She worked on me and worked on me, and I kept saying no. Then she finally came to me and she said, "Listen, Bob. I found this great little duplex. Its owner occupied on one side with a tenant on the other side, so the owner really fixed it up nice. The property is for sale by owner. We can get it a decent deal. It'll cash flow after we get a mortgage on it. You won't have to deal with it. I will manage it. I just need your support because if I don't do this I'm going to regret this rest of my life and you wouldn't want that, would you?" I mean, come on, what do you say to that?

Shannon:
You say, "You know, honey, I think we should get into real estate."

Bob:
I said, "You're absolutely right, but if this thing goes south I don't know if I'll be able to resist saying I told you so."

About a year later we were taking a look at the property's rents and depreciation schedule. All I could think was, "Holy smokes, we've got somebody living in our investment property who works all month long to make sure that we're the first one that gets paid. What an amazing business model." Then we get all these tax write offs, and the property was appreciating in value. This is phenomenal! It was one of those moments where I was like, "Wow, I'm glad I thought of it."

Shannon:
So when you were sitting in that real estate office, did she turn to you and say, "I told you so," or did she just say, "Bob, I am so glad you thought of this."

Bob:

You know, it's funny, Holly was really good about it. She just said, "You know what? You just needed to see it. You just needed to see it and do it," and she was right. All I could think to say was that we need to be doing a whole heck of a lot more of this, and that's what started our real estate investing career.

Back then we were so green, so naïve, we didn't understand real estate. We didn't understand wholesale buying opportunities. We did what 99.9 percent of the investors in this country do: go out, find a property, pay almost full price for it, put a tenant in the darn thing, and then you pray and hope that it's going to cash flow sometime in the next ten years. That's where our investing career started, but it gave me the bug and I had a desire to learn more, to grow in that business, to learn creative real estate strategies so that I could acquire properties for pennies on the dollar or buy them without any money out of pocket. I understood that with the right knowledge and drive to be a successful investor, I would never have to worry about money again.

Shannon:

Now, you've got all this knowledge and you've got years of experience, if someone wanted to get started in real estate, what would you recommend is the very first thing they do?

Bob:

The very first thing they need to do is get educated. That's just it. It's a business whereby if you know what you're doing you can make a whole lot of money and if you don't you can lose a whole lot of money. There is absolutely no ceiling on your income—the sky's the limits. You can become a millionaire, a billionaire, and I'm sure that down the road there will even be trillionaire real estate investors. The problem is, there's no floor either.

Shannon:

Yeah, I guess, if there's no ceiling...

Bob:

Yeah, if you don't know what you're doing, you can lose money. That's the biggest thing. You've got to get educated so that you have at least a common baseline of information, so you know how to fall in love with the deal and not the property. You need to know how to work the numbers and ensure that you are making a good, prudent business decision that's going to be profitable for you. The next thing is you've got to take action. I see too many individuals who fall into the category of what I call, educated derelicts. They're so versed on all sorts of different real estate strategies and different ideas, but they don't do anything with it. It's just fear that holds them back.

Shannon:
What do you do to get over that fear?

Bob:
Again, get educated. Education builds competency and when you feel competent about something you are more likely to take action. Action helps you to overcome fear, so the real formula for success is for a person to get educated and then to get busy. Education without action will not produce results.

For example, there are three types of students: the drop outs, the graduates, and the eternal. Those who keep learning and never start applying what they have learned continue to make up a larger and larger segment of our population. They are paralyzed by fear. Let me give you an old acronym for fear

False
Evidence
Appearing
Real.

I believe that wealth is a mindset. Individuals start a conversation in their own mind that leads them to a certain belief, that belief either prevents them from moving forward or actually compels them to move forward. How they see risk plays an important role. Somewhere in their internal dialogue is a conversation about risk. When their focus shifts to all that can go wrong with an opportunity, they talk themselves out of moving forward with that opportunity.

That's why we build local communities of real estate investors all across the country. These local groups get together on a regular basis to talk about their real estate deals and what's going on in their business. When you've got somebody brand new who is fearful about fixing and flipping or building cash flow, it makes all the difference in the world to immerse them in an active community of investors. Surrounded by investors who are making offers, doing deals, and making money, a student gains confidence to make it happen for themselves.

At Renatus, we surround our students with examples of success so that they can get a realistic view of what it takes to succeed. In colleges and universities, students are stuck on the degree treadmill. They risk nothing and just keep going from class to class to class and degree to degree to degree. The lack of real world experience is the challenge with higher education.

Shannon:

Which becomes their new job.

Bob:

Yeah. It's not until they get into the real world that they start to experience anything. Believe me, I am a big proponent of education in whatever form that it can possibly come from. Unfortunately, higher education is letting more people down. They're getting degrees in fields of study that they will never make a living in and sometimes it enables them to just stay in that "safe" environment where they never take action which is why student loan debt continues to increase and student outcomes continue to decrease.

Shannon:

So, how do you change that?

Bob:

Specialized knowledge. It's unfortunate that the world of academia will never accept our type of educators because many of them don't have a college degree. Heck, some of them barely got their GED, but they are all successful, profitable investors. As for me, I got right into the world of business and by the time my friends were all graduating from college, I was making two to three times the money they were making.

Shannon:

How did you get educated? What did you do?

Bob:

You're going to love this story. I started my career in sales and marketing and then because of the frustration I dealt with working for someone else, I stepped into the wonderful world of owning and operating my own businesses. I had learned over the years how to build training platforms. I knew how to build sales teams. I knew how to create and build companies and I had a business partner who was also a seasoned entrepreneur. Together we were involved in a travel company but, after 9/11, nobody wanted to talk about travel; everybody was hunkered down and fearful of getting around the world. Our travel business really tanked. I did about everything I possibly could to get the wings back on the plane and make that thing fly again, but it just wasn't happening.

It was at that point that I had a conversation with my partner. I said, "Listen. Sometimes the best way to protect an opportunity is to create a new one." We owned real estate but we didn't understand wholesale buying or a lot about the real estate industry. I suggested we create an educational company centered on real estate investing. Then we hired the big gurus to come in and teach our people how to invest. The idea was that while our students learned, we would learn. What an idea, right?

That's where it all started. But the challenge was that the gurus we hired to teach students, students who paid good money to be in those classes, often refused to teach! They only wanted to whet the appetite of the listener so that they could up sell them to their own courses.

Shannon:
Oh, wow.

Bob:
So I talked to a friend of mine who had a PhD in Education. I told him we had a problem we needed to get beyond. Somehow we had to create a true learning environment instead of the ridiculous circus sales environment that our competitors used. He said he could help and we hired him.

He worked with us, and our staff, very closely for about a year. We brought in subject matter experts (SMEs) to help us take a good look at the real estate industry and construct our curriculum. We went out and organized focus groups from those who had paid money to gurus, both those who had and had not invested yet. All those focus groups assisted us in understanding what holds people back from investing.

We found there were four principle reasons for not investing: I don't have the time, I don't have the money/credit, I don't have the knowledge, or I'm just afraid. Those were the most common excuses. I view them as the excuses that cause failure.

Shannon:
I think we can say that for every aspect of our lives.

Bob:
Yes, we can. As soon as you start doing something, all of a sudden you say, "Hey, that wasn't so bad." I liken it to people who are W-2 employees. Most are fearful about whatever new thing they take on in life. For example, let's go back to the first day they started a new job or a new career. Were they a little intimidated? Were they a little nervous? If they're honest, they're always going to say yes. Fast forward six months. By then they have a pretty good handle on it. Most would say that they had gotten really good at their job and feel confident in it. The challenge is that they rarely ever feel like they are getting paid what they are worth?

We all go through that process. Fear is overcome through action. We've got to get people in an environment that helps them to take one step after another. That's another thing I learned from Dr. Paul Ripicke. He taught us about the Instructional System design (ISD) methodology for curriculum building. It's what every major college and university in the country uses to build their curriculum paths and focus on student outcomes. We thought, "well, if Harvard and Yale and Princeton are using this, we can use it too," so we went out and worked with individuals who were actual full-time investors in a specific strategy and we brought them on board. We worked with them to help us craft these classes, and then we taught them how to teach, and then we fired all the gurus. From that point forward, we had real-life investors standing up in front of our classrooms teaching our students. We forbid any of those instructors to ever sell anything in class because we knew that that would be a massive conflict of interest because the minute they started selling they would stop teaching.

Shannon:
Was there one type of person or personality that seemed to be most drawn to your classes or had the type of personality to be the most successful?

Bob:
It's not the personality, it's the circumstance. That's the one thing that all of our students shared; there was a heightened level of dissatisfaction with where they were. It didn't matter whether they were in a successful profession or they were just out of college struggling to make ends meet. They all had a level of dissatisfaction, whether it was enough time with their family, or a good enough future, or they were just sick and tired of working for a boss that didn't appreciate them. They all had a level of dissatisfaction. Again, wealth is a mind-set. We just needed to give them hope.

Even for the staff who work here at Renatus, there's a huge shift in their mental framework. They may come in believing they need to contribute each month to their 401(k), but they end up learning how to do creative real estate investing to build their own wealth that they can control. It's pretty exciting to see that the staff members are also embracing the classes and getting out and doing their own deals.

Shannon:
It's kind of exciting because your employees could turn into full-time real estate investors and then you get to hire new employees and teach them, wouldn't you think?

Bob:
You know, there's always that thought in the back of your mind that, key people are going to start making so much money they're going to leave you. I encourage it, but over and over and over again I've got that same group of people who say, "You know what? This is what I want to do for the rest of my life," Renatus is a cause more than it is a job to them because they see the benefits that are showing up in other people's lives and that gives them a great deal of self-satisfaction.

Shannon:
Do you think students should find one real estate investing strategy and stick with that and become an expert, or do you think they should diversify?

Bob:
One of our favorite classes is understanding your investor ID because everybody's different. For example, some individuals have no problem going out there and buying property that they're going to put

lower-income tenants into. They're just happy to get that check from the government every single month. Other individuals believe that if they wouldn't live in it, then they won't own it. We have different types of personalities and mindsets. They can all make money in real estate.

What we've got to do is figure out what their investor ID is: do they want quick turn real estate for lump sum cash returns or do they want to build cash flow over time with a nice, passive income from the property? I always tell people, once you figure out your investor ID, then you learn everything you possibly can about that strategy and you focus on that to become an expert.

But, you never stay stuck with just one strategy because markets shift and change. That's why we teach so many different strategies in Renatus. No matter what is happening with the market, no matter what is happening with the economy, if there's a shift or an adjustment in the real estate business and you haven't secured yourself with an understanding of different ways to get the same thing done, you're going to find yourself on the outside looking in and saying, "Well, gee, the economy's bad, so, the opportunity's gone." Not true, my educated students crushed it through the Great Recession. They made money hand over fist while everybody else was bellyaching and moaning that there wasn't an opportunity out there.

Shannon:
Do you have personally a favorite acquisition strategy? Which strategy just makes you the most excited?

Bob:
You know what, I love subject to, but this strategy died during the recession because equity went away and home owners owed more than the property was worth. When I started Renatus, over five years ago, I created a three-hour training series called "Fast Track to Financial Freedom." I showed individuals exactly what was going on in the marketplace, how they could capitalize on what was taking place at that time with real estate investing, and shared with them that we were about 5.2 million homes short of where we needed to be as a nation just to maintain the demand of housing for the increased population.

Many builders do not build in a recession; some went out of business and would need to ramp back up. This would not be an immediate fix. By the time you find raw land, go through all the entitlements, sometimes dealing with the city, and put a foundation in and start putting sticks up to frame the house, you're eighteen to twenty-four months out. It's not like this is just an immediate fix. You don't go, "Oh, there's a demand. I think I'll build a house here." It's going to take a while. I believed that once we got to the backside of the recession, there would be a great housing shortage and that housing short

The good news is that the subject to real estate market has come back as prices have increased; we've seen a wild swing. Subject to is a great strategy because it's one of the best ways to acquire multiple properties and not be limited by banks and financial institutions. If you're dependent on conventional lending, you're going to be very, very limited in the amount of real estate you can do and the types of real estate transactions you can do. That's why I love a subject to–it's a great no money down strategy.

Shannon:

What about seller financing? If you're not relying on the banks, are seller financing and subject to the same thing?

Bob:

Well, yes and no. Some might refer to it as another form of seller financing because you are keeping the existing mortgage in place. Generally, seller financing is when a homeowner has a large equity position and they have the ability to create terms for the buyer to make the purchase.

Subject to is when you get the deed to the property, and you become the owner. It's yours. You own it subject to the existing mortgage, but the mortgage still stays in the name of the seller and they stay on the mortgage while you now own and control the home. Now, obviously, you've got to make sure that those payments are made, otherwise the lender will foreclose on the home and even though you're the new owner, they'll take it away from you just like they would have taken it away from the previous owner.

Shannon:

Is a subject to extremely risky as opposed to a standard seller finance, or are they about the same?

Bob:

Oh, no. When we discuss risk we have to think of who's at risk? The seller or the buyer? Individuals looking at selling their home using a subject to' are really in some serious financial stress and they know that a foreclosure on their credit rating weighs heavier against them than bankruptcy.

Individuals that are stuck in that kind of a situation want to solve that problem before that property goes to auction and the foreclosure is complete. A smart investor will reinstate the loan and purchase the property subject to the existing mortgage. That way, a subject to helps the seller get back on track as far as reestablishing their credit, and it just takes a huge weight off of them. All the stress, all the burden, all the phone calls, all the challenges. It just takes it away so they can get a fresh start and go out and do their thing. The downside for the seller is what happens if the investor who bought the property doesn't make the mortgage payments.

Shannon:

That was my next question.

Bob:

Yep. What happens? Is there a risk? Well, absolutely there's a risk because then that seller could find themselves right back in foreclosure again. Of course, it's no different than the mess they were in to begin with so they're kind of back in the same position. But the bottom line is no investor that is really worth their salt is going to buy a property, put money into that property, and then lose that property because they aren't willing to make the payments. There's a level of assurance that everything's going to happen the way that it should happen.

Now as to the risk to the investor, it's pretty small. Worst case scenario you just walk away from the deal or give it back to the original seller and, if you haven't put any improvements into the property, you're not out anything. If you had put improvements in the property and for some reason you don't have the money to make those monthly mortgage payments, well, then shame on you, you're going to lose the money that you put into the property. Of course, an educated investor would just rent the dang thing out. Then you get a tenant making the mortgage payments for you. There's always a way if you know what you're doing.

Shannon:

That feeds back to all the different strategies. If I, as an investor, were to be in a tough spot and I had learned everything I could learn from you, it seems like I could go to my investment group and say, "Hey, who wants this property? I need help," and they would have the knowledge to help me out.

Bob:

Yep. Absolutely. You know it's just nice to have people that have been there, done that, to be able to pick their brain and lean on them from time to time. We've developed a really unique culture inside of Renatus. It's a culture of servant leadership, meaning that you never, ever ask anybody to do something you wouldn't be willing to do yourself.

If somebody in the community needs help and assistance then we have a pay it forward kind of mentality; but what I see from an awful lot of real estate groups out there, especially a lot of real estate groups, is that they're very motivated to try and maximize their relationships inside the club. There's so many investors in those things that are just looking to prey on brand new investors. They tell them they have a fantastic property that they could turn around and rehab and sell and make 50 grand, but they have to hand over a $10,000 assignment fee to get it.

Then, the brand new greenie goes and buys the property because some seasoned guy said it was going to be a great deal, and they find out that the price they bought it for was over-inflated, the supposed selling price was also over-inflated, and now they're going to lose money on the deal because they didn't know how to work the numbers for themselves. In our community, we apply a lot of emphasis on our leaders and on others in the company to make sure that we take care of community members because they're going to be with us for life.

With that continued emphasis, I outline for them how a deal should be done: Do not sell property to people in the community, unless we want to become a business partner with them, form an LLC with an operating agreement, and have exit strategies already spelled out; do not loan money to anybody in the community or borrow money from anybody in the community unless you become business partners, again with an operating agreement.

That helps to minimize risk. I hate organizations whereby brand new, especially green or naïve individuals get taken advantage of because they think that somebody is trustworthy. You must do your own due diligence because no one is going to care about your financial wellbeing as much as you.

Shannon:

You know, that is so unique to your organization and I love it. If more people just lived their life that way, not just in real estate but just lived their life that way, our world would be so incredibly different.

Bob:

We are all about student outcomes. When somebody buys an educational package from us, after the first year, if they're in good standing with the company, we convert them over to complimentary lifetime access. That means that they're going to have access to refreshed or improved and updated classes given to them for free, for life.

If we have new classes and new material that we roll out to the field, we just give it to our students, again without any additional charge. The complimentary lifetime access is a very, very coveted feature of the Renatus educational system.

Shannon:

You've done a lot of amazing things. You've built businesses, you've adapted, you're married, you have children, you have thousands of people that you mentor and that look up to you every day. What type of legacy to you want to make sure that you leave for them?

Bob:

Let me explain my motivation. The reason why I tick the way I tick, and believe me it's taken a lot of self-evaluation to figure it out, is that when I was a kid I had a father who was an alcoholic and a drug addict. His addictions created an enormous amount of financial stress in the home because we didn't know where our next meal was going to come from or what we would do when the power was turned off. I remember the bishop of our church was kind enough, when we lived behind him, to run an extension cord from his house over to our house so that we could run the refrigerator and watch Saturday morning cartoons after the power and the utilities had been turned off.

There was a lot of financial stress. I was a little kid and I didn't really understand it at that point, but as I started to grow it became more evident. The best thing that ever happened to Dad and the family was when he got caught for check fraud. That's what happens with addicts. They lie, they steal and they cheat, so that they can feed their addiction. Best thing that ever happened to him was he went away to jail for two years. Prison was a forced rehab for him.

When he was sober my Dad was a pretty brilliant guy. He graduated top of his class from University of Pennsylvania, and he went on to get his law degree from there. He was an assistant district attorney in San Francisco and had his own private practice up in Seattle. I mean, he was a smart guy. It was just addiction had taken a toll.

The other thing that meant a lot to me was my church, my faith. I served a two-year mission for my church. I loved every minute of it, being able to teach people how to apply gospel principles to bring them a lot of joy and happiness was rewarding. When you take that kind of philosophy and those correct principles and you put them into business with an investment like real estate, you can teach people a career path that will give them security, stability, financial freedom, and independence. You allow them to then give back to the community and to the world, and you can leave your kids and grandkids a lasting legacy from the inheritance they'll receive when you finally finish your time on this planet.

For me, all of that really has kind of led me to where I'm at today. My greatest satisfaction comes from seeing our students actually do what we teach them how to do and succeed. It comes from seeing them be good stewards of the money that they make. That's another thing, I'm not one of these flashy guys. I've got a nice house and I've got some nice cars, but I'm not driving around in a million-dollar Lamborghini.

There's not a lot of the flash and the bling and the nonsense with me because I don't want to set a bad example for my team. I would rather talk to them about cash flow. I would rather talk about assets. I would rather talk about balance sheets and profit and loss statements and how they can improve their lives and what they're doing to improve the lives of others. If I can make an impact on the community that really transforms their way of thinking so that they act and behave in that manner, we'll change the world.

What brings me the greatest amount of happiness is that I love seeing the positive changes in people's lives. In my first real estate company I dealt with a business partner who lost his focus. His ego got out of hand and he forgot about the people. It was all about his ego and his own self-aggrandizement. His world got so big that he just found himself working harder and harder to feed the monster of his creation. He had an enormous house and expensive cars and private servants and nannies and security details. He even had a jet.

I was just so disappointed with him; he set a bad example for the team. A lot of people in the community wanted to be like him. They started to make really bad financial decisions and leverage themselves into cars and houses and things that weren't producing income for them. He ended up filing for bankruptcy and had to liquidate millions in personal debt.

But life was always good for me because I've always lived well below my means. There's a massive lesson in that. Be a good steward of what you've got, live below your means, and you can still enjoy life, and I do. I enjoy life, and I don't have financial stress, and if everything but my real estate was taken away from me today I would still make a really nice income and never have to worry about money the rest of my life. I want people to have what I have. That's why I do what I do.

Michael Andrews

Michael Andrews is a creative marketing professional with 26 years of sales, marketing, and communication management experience. He was a real estate agent for 15 years, working in top sales offices, and has also built and renovated homes in Maryland and Georgia. As a real estate investor, he has completed multiple residential and commercial projects. At this time, he's actively working on real estate projects in the state of Florida. He is a facilitator of a national real estate group and is working to expand to all 50 states, as well as being a part in the growth of 40,000 members nationwide. Michael is a top-notch trainer and helps others to do wholesaling, fix & flip deals, rehabbing, buy & hold strategies, and credit restoration. He also helps others to use their self-directed IRAs for real estate. He is a well-known and sought-after speaker, at local and national levels, who brings a high degree of powerful energy to his talks. He excels in effectively leading cross functional teams towards high levels of achievement. He has built teams of 3,000 members in 90 days, helping the company to hit the $100,000,000 mark in 2013. He has had multiple businesses and has run them successfully, including a construction company, therapeutic massage facility, car dealership, high-end clothing store, and an online store. Michael also enjoys mentoring and taking time to talk to youths about financial literacy and topics such as credit, balancing a checkbook, investing, and starting their own company so they can get a head start in life.

Shannon:

According to Forbes magazine, real estate is one of the top three ways people become wealthy. As a real estate expert, why do you feel this is the case?

Michael:

Well, that's the case because it is one of the quickest ways to become a self-made millionaire and billionaire. If you look at the purchase price of homes that people are acquiring today, being able to create a profit off of those sales really leads to people being able to have massive income, and even passive income. So, it's very attractive. If you look at selling a cup of coffee, selling a soda, or health products you're not going to get the same profit margins. If you sell a house or commercial building you're going to have a much higher profit margin, and it will consistently be that way.

Shannon:

What inspired you to get started in real estate?

Michael:

What inspired me to get into real estate is what was stated in the Forbes article: real estate is one of the top three ways to become wealthy. Also my mother inspired me at a young age to look into real estate as a career. It was a way for me to spend time with my wife and family, to be able to get out of debt, have a passive income, and have a great lifestyle and the freedom you need to really enjoy your life. I watched many people have success in real estate and enjoying their life styles and their passions, and I wanted to do the same thing.

Shannon:

How has your education in real estate changed the way that you invest?

Michael:

Education changed the way that I invest because it minimized the mistakes, the traps, the pitfalls that so many succumb to. Education can enhance your confidence, and if you have a mentor they can help you by holding your hand through the process.

Shannon:

What is one of the top real estate strategies that you have learned?

Michael:

One of the top real estate strategies that I've learned is fix and flip. Right now Realty Track Data shows that you can make an average profit of $58,081 in the United States. The median household income per year, according to data from the US Census, is $56,516. One deal a year puts you above the average earning in a household. It's also not too hard to learn. Once you learn the process, you can create some very good income.

Shannon:

If someone was going to get started in real estate, what would you recommend they do first?

Michael:

I would recommend they start with wholesaling, I call it "selling paper." You don't have to have credit, funds, or money down to do it. It's a quick way to get paid within 30 days. That's very attractive.

Shannon:

How has real estate changed your life?

Michael:

Well again, it's changed my life because it allows me to spend every day with my wife and that's something that I was really interested in when I looked at this career. I wanted to find something that could help me enjoy my lifestyle and be able to spend time with my family and travel. Providing financial security is extremely important to me, and real estate has been the vehicle to accomplish this.

Shannon:

In your business, how do you help other people learn more about real estate?

Michael:

My business partners and I created a local platform that allows beginners, intermediates, advanced, and experts to come together. This is where we're able to mastermind and learn more about real estate. The synergy between each individual helps us to accomplish our goals and creates energy in our community here in Florida. We're truly excited about helping many people.

Shannon:
What are some creative ways to acquire a property?

Michael:
One creative way to acquire property is seller financing. Other ways that are creative to acquire property are through self-directed IRAs, HELOC, business line of credit, and life insurance. There are a lot of different ways that you can use these tools to be able to get into real estate in a good way.

Shannon:
If you're starting with little money or poor credit, what are some strategies to get into real estate?

Michael:
So again, that would be wholesaling. Wholesaling allows you to find a property and analyze it and then be able to move the property over to a person that would actually fix and flip it or even hold the property. If a person has little money and no credit, that would be the best strategy to use to get started. Then, of course, after that, there's seller financing, but you would definitely want to have the education to know how to do those.

Shannon:
I'd like to actually go back to the creative ways to acquire a property. You talked about the creative acquisitions like seller financing and self-directed IRAs, but how do you find those properties?

Michael:
So, there are many tools out there. We have a specific tool that allows us to navigate and find properties. Another way to do it would be to look at pre-foreclosures. Pre-foreclosures are a great way to find people who are extremely motivated and want to find a way to either keep their property or sell their property without hurting their credit by moving it to foreclosure or bankruptcy. That would be a great way using pre-foreclosures and also people who are leaving town because of their jobs. There's a lot of great opportunities out there, such as people who are in a divorce and they're looking for a way to get out. You can go through seller financing and be able to use that strategy to have them basically hold the note and then you're able to create a

way to have payments go to them and also have a way that people can come and be able to rent the property or whatever it may be to get out of that transaction.

Shannon:
What is the number one mistake an individual makes when buying their first investment property?

Michael:
The number one mistake, I would say, is only having one exit strategy. Everyone should have three exit strategies for every transaction. We say that people should have three ways in and three ways out. Most first-time investors make the mistake of only having one way in and one way out.

Shannon:
Do you have a favorite investment strategy for going in?

Michael:
Yes. My favorite investment strategy, because I'm looking at holding properties, is lease option. I really like a lease option because it's different than rent because the people who do lease options have the option to buy the house. Typically, in that situation they know that they're going to become owners of that house, which means they're not going to trash your property which is one of the biggest issues that people have. A lot of times I'm looking at going into deals and then doing a lease option with an individual that may not have the best credit or may have a job where they're 1099. It's a very attractive way and it also allows you to save in taxes.

Shannon:
When you began your real estate investing career, how important was it for you to establish a team to help you be successful?

Michael:
Well, it's detrimental not to have an established team. If you don't have a great team, your success is very limited. You have to have an established team. You need to interview the team. You need to make sure you ask them questions that allow you to know that they've been doing it, they're experienced. This would allow you to leverage their

education, time, and resources so that you don't always have to know everything about every single aspect of real estate. You'll have people that can help you through the process.

Shannon:

How have mentors, in your real estate investing, helped you navigate potential pitfalls?

Michael:

That's exactly what it is, it's a pitfall. Mentors have helped me to steer around those pitfalls by letting me know that if you're going in a certain direction that's not favorable, they can use their past experiences to help you. Their experiences, good or bad, can help you to make sure that you are doing the strategy properly.

Shannon:

Do you have a specific time when a mentor has helped you that you would like to share?

Michael:

Yes. Michael Poggi, a personal friend & business partner of mine that has been in real estate for over 20 years. I was starting a rehab on one of my projects, and he helped understand it was important to make sure that my contractor was there daily. I was not aware at the time before I got this training that a lot of contractors go from project to project. They could be working on your project and six others at the same time. Due to the knowledge that he gave me to make sure that the contractor was there daily, I was able to finish the project in 45 days instead of 90 days. That significantly decreased my holding fees. The value of a mentor is priceless!!!

Shannon:

What advice would you give to someone who is allowing fear to hold them back from starting their real estate investing?

Michael:

I would tell them to join a local real estate group and be part of their property tours. These events will help you build confidence. When you're at these events you can align yourself with people that can help you through the process. Then you will be ready to build a powerful team and minimize your fears to get you over the hurdles that you may run into.

Shannon:
Do you feel that real estate investing success is dependent on a strong economy?

Michael:
No. Really, it's just the opposite. Some of the most powerful opportunities came between 2008 and 2010. It was the biggest exchange of wealth that I was around to experience. If you were liquid and had money at that time, you would have had opportunities to get 10 to 100 to 1000 properties during that period of a time for pennies on the dollar. Really, good economies and bad economies are both good to be involved in. You just have to have the education to know what to do during those times.

Shannon:
How does learning multiple investing strategies protect and accelerate your investing success?

Michael:
If you take 2008 as an example, most people had one way in and one way out when they were doing real estate transactions. If you have multiple strategies, it allows you to minimize your risk because if the property ends up being over cost when you're doing your rehab, you can hold the property and then wait for the market to catch up and then enjoy the cash flow. Then you can sell the property, so you want to have multiple strategies just in case there are mistakes that happen during a process, or unforeseen occurrences. It also allows you to make extra income per deal. Each strategy will allow you to earn extra income.

Shannon:
What is cash flow and why should it be such an important focus of your business?

Michael:
Cash flow is the amount that is transferred into and out of your business. Why it's so important for your business is because it's the

bloodline of the success of your business. It allows you to diversify your portfolio; it allows you to be able to get into buy and hold strategy. It allows you to create passive income and do commercial real estate as well and then you'll have all the more cash flow.

Shannon:

How does real estate allow you to earn massive and passive income?

Michael:

Massive income is gained on the price of each real estate transaction. In the United States, we get an average of $58,081 per rehab deal, which is amazing. Also, if you have a buy and hold and you're holding a property, you're able to make monthly income every single month. I call it "mailbox money." So, every single month that comes in and that can be great for cash flow.

Shannon:

Can you learn everything you need to know about real estate from the local library?

Michael:

No. I think that's why many people do not become successful in real estate, because it's really about someone being there to hold your hand through the process and make sure that you know what you're doing. It's about having that team that really gets you through the process. Just going to the library and reading information really won't help you to become successful in real estate, truthfully.

Shannon:

When doing fix and flips, what's the number one thing you want to look out for?

Michael:

One of the biggest concerns in fix and flips is rehab costs. Having a good GC (General Contractor) or contractor who can tell you the true cost is very important. You want to make sure that you're also able to know if homes in the area are selling fast because your holding fees will eat your profits.

Shannon:
When doing a short sale, what should you look out for? What should you anticipate?

Michael:
You have to anticipate time. Short sales take time. Just to sell a house often 91 days, so you have to make sure you give yourself the time to know that you won't be able to sell that house for 91 days. Sometimes, to close a short sale, it might take six months just to be able to actually acquire the property, and then you have to fix it and flip it, so, you're looking at a possible six months to a year just to finish that short sale and three months would be the fastest.

Shannon:
If someone wanted to invest in multi-family dwelling, what do they need to know?

Michael:
They need to definitely get education because with multi-family, definitely, the costs are higher. You need to make sure you have strategies going into the deal that will help assist you to make sure that you are not buying the property at too high of a price but also that you have a good management team or you've taken management to make sure that the property stays rented.

Shannon:
How can a real estate investor benefit from notes, tax liens, and deeds?

Michael:
I really enjoy notes because the benefit on the notes is that you can actually make money without having to have contractors, deal with termites, and other issues that may come up, like a person not paying their rent. It's very attractive because you're creating money. It's like you're the bank in this particular case. With tax liens you're able to take benefit of the interest that you can make, regardless if you have ownership of the property.

Shannon:
Most millionaires and billionaires have invested in commercial real estate. Why do you think that is?

Michael:

During down economies, you still can create income during those times. It's great to have commercial real estate in your portfolio because, during those times, everybody that may have lost their job, or may have lost their credit, they look for apartments. They look for opportunities to be able to find a place to stay. Commercial real estate will always be there for them.

Shannon:

What type of legacy do you want to leave?

Michael:

I want to leave a legacy like my father did. He acquired 560 acres of land, which included several homes and buildings. My focus is to add more land, more residential, more commercial deals to our family legacy. To maintain the lifestyle that I really feel my family deserves.

Amy & BirdDog Berteaux

Amy and BirdDog Berteaux are exceptional real estate investors. Both are military veterans and have taken the skills they acquired from being leaders in the military to entrepreneurs and real estate investors in the civilian world to show them how to achieve their dreams. They have learned how to choose and pick the partnerships they need to make things happen and succeed in real estate.

Amy was raised in Utah for most of her life and has always dreamed of investing in real estate. She is the third of six kids. Her father had invested in real estate when she was little and made good money doing it but never taught her how to invest. She knew real estate investing could be a lucrative way of life, one that could give her the kind of life she knew she wanted. She finally got the courage to do it when she found real estate education and learned how to whole-sale deals to other investors. Her initial partner ended up stabbing her in the back and going off on her own. Looking back, she's grateful to have experienced that because it has caused her to be a smarter and safer investor. She was also able to find a community that has changed her life and has given her the knowledge to invest in more ways other than just wholesaling properties to other investors.

BirdDog was born as Patrick Berteaux, but as a Native American he prefers to be referred to by his Native name, BirdDog. He never knew "BirdDog" was also a real estate investing term until after getting involved in real estate. BirdDog is the eighth of nine children and his family moved frequently around California, Texas, and Washington state. He finally settled in Utah unexpectedly, and that is where he ended up meeting Amy. He was only temporarily stationed in her unit, but ended up back in her unit a couple other times after that initial temporary time. It took him three years till he finally got her committed to a relationship.

Amy and BirdDog have been married for going on three years and have three beautiful children. They are truly looking forward to their lives as they continue to build for them and their children. Since getting involved in real estate together, their lives have been so much better and full of experiences and lots of friends that invest with them.

Shannon:

According to Forbes magazine, real estate is one of the top three ways people become wealthy. As a real estate expert, why do you feel this is the case?

BirdDog:

Because it's very lucrative and it's the quickest way to actually make money by fixing and flipping and buy and hold. You can actually pay for retirement that way instead of relying on the government.

Shannon:

When you're looking for a house to flip, what is the first thing you look for?

BirdDog:

Whether it has meth in it, because then I can get a discount price.

Shannon:

Amy, after BirdDog checks for the meth, what is the first thing you look for doing a fix and flip?

Amy:

I run the numbers and make sure the numbers work. The numbers work, then it's good. If they don't work, it doesn't matter what it is.

Shannon:

If someone is starting with little money or poor credit, what are some strategies that they can use to get into real estate?

Amy:

Our favorite is 'subject to.' The other one would be utilizing other investors' money.

Shannon:

When you began your real estate investing career, how important was it for you to establish a team to help you be successful?

Amy:

It was very important. We had to make sure we had contacts, contractors, mentors, friends that have done it before.

BirdDog:
Your success is based upon other people's success. You want to line yourself up to where you're going to succeed, so you need a team to build your net worth and your empire.

Amy:
So he tried to say your network is your net worth.

Shannon:
How have mentors in your real estate investing helped you navigate potential pitfalls?

Amy:
They've been able to give us insight or experience. Insight, I guess.

BirdDog:
On the more experience part, that we don't know.

Shannon:
What inspired you guys to get into real estate?

BirdDog:
My wife.

Amy:
It's always been something I've wanted to do. My dad was into real estate, but he never taught me how to do it. It's just been something I've always wanted.

Shannon:
If someone were going to want to get started in real estate and they came to you, what would you recommend they do first?

BirdDog:
Get properly educated—knowledge.

Amy:
Education is critical—knowledge.

BirdDog:
Knowledge is power, but applied knowledge is even more.

Shannon:
How has your education changed the way that you invest?

Amy:
We make smarter decisions.

BirdDog:
We don't run off emotions. We run off of the knowledge that we apply, like running the numbers to make sure everything's correct other than to think, 'Oh, that might work.' Everything might work, but unless the numbers work, nothing else does.

Shannon:
How can an investor benefit from a lease option?

BirdDog:
Cash flow. Cash flow is everything.

Shannon:
Okay. Expand on that. What is cash flow and why is it so important to your business?

BirdDog:
Well, cash flow is so important to my business just for the simple fact that the more money that I have coming in dictates on what I can do next. For an investor, cash flow is pretty much a rental property, renting it out for more than what it currently is. If the mortgage on the house is $1200, I'd want to lease it an additional $300 to $400 on top of it so I can have the $300 to $400 that I can put in my own pocket or to invest in a different place. That's cash flow.

Shannon:
When you're looking for homes that create that positive cash flow, do you have a minimum standard that you're looking for?

BirdDog:
$400.

Amy:
A month.

BirdDog:
A month per unit.

Shannon:
Why?

BirdDog:
Because it gives me a safety blanket in case something happens, whether a water heater goes out or something like that.

Shannon:
If someone wanted to invest in multifamily dwellings, what do they need to know?

BirdDog:
They need to know the how many units they're purchasing, how much they're purchasing it for, and also figure out what the rate of return is on the house, or on the multifamily home. If it's a 12-unit, you want to multiply the purchase price times how many doors you have divided by just depending on what it is, the percentage you want to make back on it. For each door, if you want $400, you have to divide it by $400 per door to make sure that it's the right amount for you to want to get into.

Shannon:
Do you think that multifamily dwellings are more lucrative or less lucrative than single-family homes?

BirdDog:
They're more lucrative because you're managing 12 doors instead of one.

Shannon:
So other than it just being more doors in one place, is there anything else different that somebody would need to know about a multifamily dwelling rather than a single?

Amy:
You have to deal with the property management aspect as well.

BirdDog:
Yeah, and what their risks are and what they want to do. Every property manager's different.

Shannon:
Would you ever manage the property yourself?

Amy:
Absolutely not.

Shannon:
Why do you think it's a bad idea to manage the property yourself?

BirdDog:
The more problems you have on your table, the less you'll be able to invest because your mind is too worked up on the one property that you're working on. You're not going to want more of them. If you let a property manager manage it and do all the stuff and all you do is just get the returns on it, it's better for you because then you can go after more properties.

Amy:
Plus they're professional and they've done it. They know what they're doing.

Shannon:
What do you think is the number one mistake an individual makes when buying their first investment property?

BirdDog:
They get emotionally attached to it.

Amy:
Which ends up that they usually pay more than what they should, whether they pay more in fixing it up or pay more with buying it.

BirdDog:

Yeah. They get too excited to get into it and then they end up loving it too much to where they're putting too much money into it. Now it's the most expensive house on the block and no one wants it.

Shannon:

What advice would you give to someone who is allowing fear to hold them back from starting their real estate investing?

BirdDog:

The more you wait, the less you make, so it's better just to do it.

Shannon:

What about you, Amy?

Amy:

I tell people don't let fear hold you back because then you're not going to be able to do anything. Take risks, as long as you're educated with what you're doing you'll be okay. Make sure you get a whole network of people you can rely on so the fear will be less. If you don't do it, you won't have that experience. You won't be able to apply it. You won't be making the money that you want to make from it. Figure out why you want to do it and make that bigger than what the fear is.

Shannon:

Do you feel that real estate investing success is dependent on a strong economy?

Amy:

No. You can do real estate investing in any economy. You just have to know what real estate strategy works in the economy that you're in.

Shannon:

What is a good example of a strategy to use to acquire a property in a strong economy?

BirdDog:

I go after NODs. That's my choice. Right now, we're in a great market. The houses are well above what I want to pay for them, so I'm more interested in going after those that are behind on their mortgages.

Shannon:

What is an NOD?

BirdDog:

A notice of default. People that are in foreclosure or about ready to go in foreclosure and don't have any exit strategies on how to get out of their home.

Shannon:

Where do you find those?

Amy:

County records and title companies

BirdDog:

There are lots of different places on where you can find it. It's about getting it as soon as possible then you can act on it. You want to definitely get it before the auction date, though.

Shannon:

How can a real estate investor benefit from tax liens and deeds?

Amy:

They get cash flow but without having to worry about tenants.

BirdDog:

It's just paperwork.

Amy:

It's just dealing with the paperwork aspect and they still get the cash flow for it.

Shannon:

When doing a short sale, what should you anticipate?

Amy:
It's going to take a long time.

BirdDog:
It takes forever. Up to a year, if not...

Amy:
It could be a couple years.

Shannon:
How long do they usually take from beginning to end?

Amy:
It varies, but I want to say a year to three years, typically. It depends on how motivated the bank is. A lot of times they just ...

BirdDog:
Sit on.

Amy:
Sit on it.

BirdDog:
They want to get rid of it, but at the same time, they don't know what to do with it. So they sit on it for a year or two years, three years, or it just falls through the crack and they forget about it.

Shannon:
Amy, how has real estate changed your life?

Amy:
It's given me the time to spend with my family. It's given me a different lifestyle, one that I can actually enjoy with my family.

Shannon:
BirdDog, how about you?

BirdDog:
It increased my knowledge on the way in which money and banks actually work and run on and that I don't need my own credit, my own

money, or my own knowledge necessarily to get what I want in life. I can use other people's knowledge and skillsets to get what I want.

Shannon:
Amy, why do you think that most people are successful at real estate?

Amy:
They get educated one way or another so they know what they're doing and they don't make stupid or uneducated decisions.

Shannon:
So exact opposite. Why do you think people fail at real estate?

BirdDog:
Knowledge.

Amy:
They don't know what they're doing. They get into it thinking, 'Oh, I can just buy a property and rent it out.' But if they don't buy it at a good price, they may not be able to get a good return on it. I hear a lot of people buying properties and then renting them out and having to pay money in order to keep it going because they didn't buy it at the right amount.

Shannon:
Other than notice of defaults, what are some creative ways that you guys have used to acquire properties?

Amy:
Subject to. Using the existing mortgage that's in place. That's our favorite strategy to use.

BirdDog:
That's our really only favorite. That deal is about the only one that we do use.

Amy:
We'll use other investors as well.

Shannon:

Why do you think subject to is your favorite? Most of the time people have a reason for why they like something and why they don't. Why do you think subject to is your favorite?

BirdDog:

The least risk.

Amy:

Yeah. It comes with the least amount of risk because you need the least amount of money out of pocket. Then you can go around, hold onto it for six months and fix it up and then flip it. It's all depending on what you negotiate with the homeowners, whether you hold it for a short term, whether you hold it for a long term. It's definitely less risky to hold it for a short term and fix it and flip it. You can end up holding it long term if you negotiate that with the homeowner as long as you do your due diligence with them to minimize your own risk of losing it.

Shannon:

Okay, so you're using someone else's mortgage and someone else's money. Is there a risk to a real estate investor for loss when doing a subject to?

Amy:

Yes. If the homeowner ends up filing bankruptcy, the house could be tied up in that bankruptcy and you could lose that house and everything you put into it. That's why you want to make sure you do your due diligence with the homeowners to make sure they're not going to be filing bankruptcy for as long as you're going to be utilizing their mortgage. That's the most risky aspect. That's where you need to make sure you're talking and communicating with the homeowner that they don't have extra debts as well.

BirdDog:

And why you also only want to do it for six months to a year because once you fix it and then flip it, it gets everyone out of the agreement. It's already on to the next person who's buying it, not anybody else's.

Shannon:
How does learning multiple investment strategies protect and build investment success?

BirdDog:
Well, the more options you have, the better a situation you have to pick up the property at a discounted price. Also, the more exit strategies you have in case something goes bad, the more likely you are to lose money.

Shannon:
Amy, what's your opinion on that?

Amy:
Oh, I just say that if you have more strategies then there's more potential you have on making money. If you go in with only saying, 'Oh, I'm going to fix and flip this house' and then the property tanks, the market changes, and that's your only exit strategy, then you're going to be losing money.

Whereas if you go in saying 'I'm going to fix and flip it, but if something happens, I still calculated enough so I could rent it out.' then you can still make monthly cash flow and then sell it once the market turns back around. Knowing multiple strategies helps you, gives you more potential on not losing money, because you could look at it different ways.

Shannon:
What type of legacy do you want to leave?

BirdDog:
A legacy that's built upon principles to help the next generation get to where they want and to be able to provide my family with enough cash flow that they never ever need any more. For generations down the road, even after I'm dead, it will still be producing. That's what I want.

Shannon:
Thank you, BirdDog. Amy, do you want to add to that?

Amy:
Yeah. I want to make sure that the legacy that I'm leaving is something that my kids and their kids would be proud of. We are teaching the next generation a legacy on how to live and how to work and how to support themselves with business and real estate so that they're not relying on other people. Because of what we've done, we can leave a legacy for our kids on what they can do.

Wanda I. Carrasquillo

Wanda I. Carrasquillo was born on the beautiful enchanted island of Puerto Rico in 1963. She was raised with high values concerning religion, education, and work ethic. She is a single mother of three, one of whom was a special needs child who passed away at the age of 28. Wanda has seven beautiful grandkids. Despite her many challenges in life, she was able to complete two Masters in Education degrees.

Though she has succeeded in her careers in many ways, she hit a glass ceiling every time she attempted to reach higher. She spent many years trading hours for money. On the side, she was always looking for business opportunities. Wanda believes she has an entrepreneurial spirit, because, as a little girl, she saw her grandparents working in their own businesses. But, she never really accomplished much in any of her business attempts.

It was not until last year that she finally found an opportunity in real estate investing. She found an educational institution where she could learn about real estate and a nationwide community of investors that support her in her efforts. She has already, with less time and effort than expected, exceeded her own income goals, as she has generated a six-figure income in eight months. She is in a dozen real estate transactions. She has been able to build a team of other entrepreneurs, allowing them to learn as she has. She feels like the future is brighter and great things are ahead of her in the years to come because she has chosen to become a real estate investor.

Shannon:

According to Forbes magazine, real estate is one of top three ways people become wealthy. As a real estate expert, why do you feel this is the case?

Wanda:

I believe that real estate will give people an opportunity to improve their income and set up a more secure retirement plan. It doesn't matter if the market goes up or down, investing in real estate is better than counting on Social Security for retirement. Real estate allows people to put their money to work for them, instead of them working for the money—which is a way to create wealth.

Shannon:

What inspired you to get into real estate?

Wanda:

I have always wanted to own apartment buildings and rental properties. Every time I drove by a big apartment complex, I asked myself 'How can I be the owner?'. I had no idea as how to get into the real estate investor's field. I also have two close friends who have rentals and I saw their lifestyle was good enough for me to pursue the same thing. The only thing was that I didn't know how to do it because I didn't have the capital. They were my inspiration and, as a matter of fact, one of them told me about courses I could take to learn how to become an investor. As a baby boomer getting closer to retirement, my fear was having to have to work for the rest of my life. I knew I needed to do something different to obtain different results. And that's why I started to look into advocating for myself and finding ways into learning how to do it.

Shannon:

If someone were to come to you and they said they wanted to get started into real estate, what would you recommend they do first?

Wanda:

My first recommendation would be to educate themselves and to find an institution where they can learn from experts. Also, to find a community of investors that can assist and support them. I attribute my success to those two components—education and community. I found both components, which allowed me to learn and have the confident to finally do it. In the community of investors, particularly, I have built relationships that have allowed me to be part of a network of people nationwide.

Shannon:
How have mentors in your real estate investing help you to navigate potential pitfalls?

Wanda:
In the community, I have found the support and confidence to know that what I'm doing, I'm doing correctly. I have found people who are mentoring me, so I don't have to go through the same errors they have made. I'm able to learn from them and not repeat the same mistakes. In my case, I'm pretty new in the field. However, the little bit that I have done, I've been really successful because I've been following their footsteps. And I've tried to copycat, if you will, their steps for me to avoid some of their mistakes.

Shannon:
In your business, how do you help others learn more about real estate?

Wanda:
I am elaborating my business in a team. A team that belongs to the bigger community. In this team, we mastermind ideas to conclude if a deal is good or bad. We review strategies learned to find ways to implement them. For my team, I'm a leader and a mentor as well. I love to share the way I have been doing real estate to empower my team members with the tools to succeed. If my team members succeed, I succeed.

Shannon:
Do you feel that real estate investing success is dependent on a strong economy?

Wanda:
Not necessarily, depending on which strategy is used. There are many strategies in the real estate arena; what matters is to learn and apply them correctly. For example, 'subject to'—it's a strategy that it

doesn't matter where the economy is at, there will always be someone losing their job, their mortgage, and with financial struggles. In which case, a real estate investor can step in to purchase the property and assist those potential sellers in these situations.

Shannon:
Tell me one strategy that is good to use in an up economy?

Wanda:
Fix and flip is a great strategy to use in a good economy because there will be more buyers. A real estate investor can purchase, fix, and sell the property in a short amount of time and work on several projects at once. I personally like fix and flips because I spend around five hours on a project for an infinite return as I don't use any of my own money to purchase or repair the homes.

Shannon:
If you are starting your real estate investing with little money or poor credit, what are some strategies that you can use to get started in real estate investing?

Wanda:
I started that way, actually! I started with very little credit and very little money. Where there is a desire to do something, there is a way to do it. In my case, I started and continue to use none of my capital or credit to purchase properties and participate on a deal. I leverage knowledge and relationships to enter in a deal. To get to this point, my greatest investment has been in my education and community. I think that investing in improving my understanding of real estate strategies and building relationships gave me the most return. It doesn't matter which credit score you have, it doesn't matter how much money you have—knowledge and relationships produce more return on investment.

Shannon:
What are some creative ways to acquire a property in a down economy?

Wanda:

In a down economy, real estate investors can use creative ways to acquire properties by finding individuals who are not paying their mortgages, getting a divorce, or going through financial hardships. As real estate investors, we can always step in to purchase those properties in a short sale or using subject to strategy. These creatives ways allow real estate investors like me to help people during hard times. Thus, it doesn't matter where the economy is as my business continues.

Shannon:

How do you feel that real estate allows you to earn massive income and passive income?

Wanda:

Right now, I'm building two streams of income--one through an incredible educational institution that allows me to generate massive income while learning real estate investing. I learn and earn at the same time because I am taking advantage of a cycle of wealth program the institution has. This program is completely optional. After I became a student at the institution, I lost my job. Using the cycle of wealth program helped me to generate a six-figure income in the first eight months. I didn't need to find another job. I just became a full-time real estate investor, and I will never look back. Now, since I've advanced on my real estate investing studies, I am applying the strategies to create a second stream of income. This is passive income for my retirement. I am basically acquiring rental properties and creating notes to increase my cash flow.

Shannon:

Explain to me about the notes strategy. How can a real estate investor benefit from notes?

Wanda:

There is a variety of ways to use the notes strategies. Once the concept is learned, using the notes strategies in real estate is easy and fun. In one of the ways, once the note is found, analyzed, and negotiated the investor connects with the broker and collects the profit. Another way is owning the note, basically, and the investor becomes the bank. This creates passive income and cash flow without having to worry about tenants, toilets, and termites.

Shannon:
What is cash flow and why should it be an important focus of your business?

Wanda:
Cash flow is the amount of money left after all business and personal obligations are met. As a business owner, increasing cash flow is important to expand my business and to do what I am more passionate about. The more cash flow, the more freedom one has to enjoy other activities. Personally, I am particularly interested about helping less fortunate people. I can actively work in this interest by having more cash flow. Cash flow is the key for financial freedom.

Shannon:
How do you feel that real estate has really changed your life?

Wanda:
Professionally, I had reached success in many ways. I had completed two Masters in Education and part of a PhD. Nonetheless, it didn't matter how committed, passionate, and excited I was about what I was doing, every time I hit a glass ceiling. A glass ceiling that didn't allow me to grow anymore. Even, with all of those years of education under my belt, I struggled financially. I had to work many hours, at times holding two jobs to be able to provide for my family as a single mother of three—one with special needs. In contrast, in this arena of real estate investing, I've found endless opportunities. In fact, in only one year and three months I have been able to complete more in less time and with less effort than ever before. Now, I have a six-figure income and have been involved in a dozen deals. In addition, I have gained more on the personal side with all the associations I have with positive people. Real estate investing changed my life for the better financially and personally.

Shannon:
Very good job—that's awesome! Okay, what is the number one mistake an individual makes when buying their first investment property?

Wanda:

I think that doing the calculations and analyzing the property before you even look at the property physically is very, very important. And if you do not do those numbers correctly, and do your quick analysis, you can enter into a deal that is not going to be a good deal. I just had an experience that we had to bail out at the closing table because it was not going to be a good deal. So yes, we lost money, but we did not lose as much as we could have, if we had ended the deal.

Shannon:

What advice would you give to someone who is allowing fear to hold them back from starting their real estate investing?

Wanda:

Many have defined fear as false evidence appearing real. Some people base their opinion on misconceptions and biases from others which is false evidence. For example, it is common to hear that real estate is risky—while there is some truth to that statement, educated people eliminate the risk factor using knowledge. Entering in the real estate field is like jumping out of an airplane: you are fearful of jumping, then once you get the instructions and confidence to jump, the fear goes away. Basically, real estate can be fearful at the beginning. Once you obtain an education and find a supporting community, the fear goes away. Don't do it alone. Do it with people that can help and provide support. That support will eliminate the fears and also will give you more confidence.

Shannon:

When doing a fix and flip, what do you want to look out for?

Wanda:

When I do a fix and flip, I want to invest in a property that allows me to give a low-income family the opportunity to live in a great property—in a property that looks like a castle, a big mansion, even if it is a small house. I do identify myself as a Walmart-type of investor. However, I make that property look like a Nordstrom property. I look for properties where I can have more potential buyers.

Shannon:

Most millionaires and billionaires have investment in commercial real estate, why do you think that is?

Wanda:

I think investing in commercial properties is very lucrative. It is a way in which passive income and cash flow increase at a faster rate. It's a faster way to capitalize knowledge and relationships and build a bigger empire.

Shannon:

I have just one question left: what type of legacy do you want to leave?

Wanda:

I'm doing this because I want to make sure that my daughters and grandkids have something to live off of, even when I'm not here. I do this because I want to help more people. I'd like to continue to build a team of individuals with a common interest in real estate that allows them to reach their goals. Also, I love to do charity. I love going to other countries to help people. With real estate, once I create more cash flow, I know that I'll be able to fulfill my passion. My dream is to impact more people in the world and to help others who are less fortunate. If I succeed, anybody can succeed. And I want to help others succeed—that's why I want to do this. I want to do this to help, not only my family and myself, but all the people in the world.

Michele L. Carson

Michele L. Carson grew up on Aquidneck Island in the seaside city of Newport, Rhode Island. She was the only girl out of a household of six brothers and was very active as a young girl. She participated in gymnastics, cross country running, roller skating, and creative dancing.

Michele attended Xavier University in New Orleans, earning a bachelor's degree in Business Administration. College was Michele's first exposure to Tae Kwon Do and Martial Arts and these are activities she continues to enjoy. After graduating from college, she moved to Maui, Hawaii, where she raised her 2 children.

Michele's main focus thus far has been getting her financial structuring in order by getting financially fit. She is a student practitioner expanding her business education and creating a positive mindset. She is intent on using her knowledge to influence her credit score and has applied little-known techniques that accelerate debt pay off. She reduced her taxes by using creative budgeting tools. Michele is learning not only to live within her means, but, more importantly, she is developing her skills and her ability to EXPAND HER MEANS by drawing from credit and increasing tax deductions.

She enjoys building new relationships and expanding her local community. She takes pleasure in assisting others in gaining control of their finances by assisting them in creating better relations with financial organizations, building strong credit profiles, and understanding the power of the 4 types of expenses.

Shannon:

According to Forbes magazine, real estate is one of the top three ways that people become wealthy. As a real estate expert, why do you feel this is the case?

Michele:

Real estate has stood the test of time. It worked 100 years ago, and it still works today, whether the market is up or down. Real estate doesn't require any licenses or degrees. There's no need for inventory or employees. It's a business you can start part time from the comfort of your home with a computer and a phone.

Real estate is a unique business because it satisfies a basic human need: the need for shelter, a place to live, the need for a home. For these reasons, real estate is the perfect ideal small business that has created wealth for so many people around the world.

Shannon:

What inspired you to get into real estate investing?

Michele:

I grew In Newport, Rhode Island, and lived a block away from many beautiful family summer mansions called The Breakers, The Vanderbilt, and The Marble House. I developed a fascination for luxurious homes and beautiful properties. I dreamed of being part of these types of homes. I loved watching Lifestyles of the Rich and Famous and figured I could do real estate without being an agent, not knowing exactly how this would happen.

My hometown of Newport was a big inspiration for my passion for real estate investing. For the longest time this dream was put on the back burner. When I did decide to branch out, I had spent several thousand dollars on several other companies' educational systems to no avail. They did not have a local support system or community to turn to. There wasn't any clear direction or guidance as to what the next steps were. This all has changed in the last 2 ½ years. Now, I am part of a local real estate community with a proven success system in place.

Shannon:

If you're starting with little money or poor credit, what are some strategies that you can use to get into real estate?

Michele:

Creative ways to get into real estate are by borrowing the money, assuming the existing mortgage, and seller financing, to name a few ways to get into a property with little of your own money and poor credit.

We're taught to negotiate the down payment amount. In fact, there is a lady in our community of investors who is known as "The Queen of $10 Down." She is very creative and has made quite a few deals with ONLY $10 as a down payment.

Shannon:

How do you find these people with money that you can invest? I'm assuming they aren't just standing out there holding a sign that says, 'Come use my money.'

Michele:

Within our community of investors we have all learned from the same proven success system so we all have the knowledge of where to find the money, where to find the deal, and how to talk to people.

There are private money lenders, hard money lenders, and there's over $23 trillion in peoples' retirement accounts that can be used to invest in real estate. We have a software system available to us that helps us match the money lender and their specific criteria with the right deal. We find the right match so it's a win-win for all involved then we can go ahead with the deal.

Shannon:

When you first began your real estate investing career, how important was it for you to establish a team to help you be successful?

Michele:

It was very important. What makes our community different from other organizations is that we work together as a team. We're not competing with each other. Having a good team to bounce ideas off of makes all the difference in the world. We're all on the same page, we're all working for the same outcome and for the same goals. We were taught the same system and have access to the same current, relevant information.

Working by yourself in real estate is very hard and risky. It's few and far between to find a "Lone Ranger" investor that is very successful.

They have no one to bounce ideas off of, and they absorb all the work and all the risk. There may be a few lucky successful solo investors out there but not very many.

Shannon:
How have members of your community or mentors in your real estate investing helped you to navigate potential pitfalls?

Michele:
When we got together during a goal session they would know if I was off-kilter, in a sense. We always want to do things that are morally correct, legal, and ethical, you want to be on the right side of the law of course, but sometimes you're just making human errors or human mistakes, and I've had people in my life that would guide me and weigh out the options. They wouldn't tell me what to do, but they would give me the different options that would be more compatible with my goals making financial sense with the best financial decision. I was able to see the big picture, and then I was able to decide which path I wanted to take; usually it was what they had suggested. Learning from other people, and getting the feedback from their experiences, makes sense.

I was hanging out with my CPA friend and team member the other day, and she was reviewing my budget. She noticed I had high credit card balances and at the same time I was overfunding my cash flow banking account. She showed me that overfunding my account at this time was costing me 22% in interest. This lead to changing the direction and reformulating a new plan for another debt pay down period.

Shannon:
Did you have a mentor that specifically worked with you on your credit?

Michele:
Yes, I did. First of all, I did my part. I studied and dove into the credit management information. I obtained a very good understanding of how credit works and what the banks are looking for in your credit report. Then, I was able to have a mentor guide me and answer my questions. I was able to I Implement what I learned, with the guidance of an experienced mentor. Their guidance helped me navigate different areas of what to do with my credit and when to make certain calculated changes to my credit.

Shannon:

If you don't mind me asking, what was your credit score when you first started investing?

Michele:

In the beginning of this journey my credit score was 596.

Shannon:

And what is your goal credit score?

Michele:

My goal is 780 and higher.

Shannon:

Great, and then what is it now?

Michele:

Right now, it is 683. That's a whopping 87-point increase in about 1 ½ years' time. However, I have a strategic plan to continue to improve my credit score since I now have control over the five factors that affect my credit score.

Shannon:

How long have you been working on this?

Michele:

I initially began working on my credit began in late 2014 with a local financial company that was helping me with budgeting and improving my credit. After a month, I was on track to upgrade to a higher package. I visited their suggested credit union to apply for a line of credit. However, I was rejected. My application for a small $5000 line of credit was totally denied.

I thought to myself 'Okay, I have a cruddy credit score,' and I came to a dead -end with this company. So, now how was I supposed to fix my credit? This company dumped me and left me high and dry. I never heard from them again. Although I was feeling very discouraged and depressed, I decided to open a checking account at that credit union anyways, in the hope that in the future things would improve. Several months later something happened. I was connected to a better company. Their system was effective, and my understanding of credit, money, and resources grew. My financial fitness has never been the same since then.

Shannon:
Isn't it amazing that when you went to where you were already partici-pating and doing business to fix your credit, that they wouldn't give you any credit?

Michele:
Yes, it was very discouraging. The credit union denied the credit ap-plication and the financial company never fixed my credit problems.

Shannon:
That really goes to show how much they believe in their own product.

Michele:
So true. I never heard from them again.

Shannon:
How does your education that you're using now for real estate change the way that you invest?

Michele:
This information, the education, has changed everything. Number one: you don't need credit to invest. Fixing my credit situation was my own personal mission that I wanted. Eventually, I want to be in a po-sition to buy a non-investment property, a luxurious home here in Maui for my family. Secondly, I know there are different banking products. There is a huge difference between lines of credits versus a loan.

I know how to pay down my bills by using velocity banking the right way. I am so excited because I'm learning what the 2%, the wealthy people in this country, teach their children. I'm not sure where they get their information from. We are blessed we have all this information, this education, all in one place. This information on money, credit, real estate and resources should be taught in our school systems today. Unfortunately, it's not.

The wealthiest 2% know how to use credit; they invest with their retirement plans, and most of them set up a 'Family Bank' with their life insurance policies. Now, I'm learning all these principles. I have so many different tools in my tool box. Our tools are information in the form of education. Our education is constantly updated; it's current, accurate, relevant, and useful, whereas other companies do not live up to such high standards.

Shannon:
Along those lines, most millionaires and billionaires have investments in commercial real estate, why do you think that is?

Michele:
It comes down to the know-how. These billionaires understand appreciation, depreciation, amortization and cash flow. They have the information, knowledge, ability, and confidence to invest in larger transactions. Commercial real estate gives more bang for their buck. It takes the same amount of time, energy, and effort to purchase one single-family home as it does to purchase an apartment complex. In a nutshell, they are buying cash flow in bulk versus buying cash flow on an individual basis, one property at a time. Billionaires have a different mindset than the average person. They have a business mindset. They are focused on replacing their earned income from their jobs and creating passive Income - or cash flow from real estate and other businesses. This creates security and financial independence. The wealthy mindset is to create wealth rapidly by controlling as many assets as possible.

Shannon:
What advice would give you someone who is allowing fear to hold them back from starting in real estate?

Michele:
It would be beneficial to find an experienced investor. They can hold your hand, lead and guide you along the way. Many first-time investors are impulsive and jump right in without knowing all the facts about the property. In March 2015, we were able to participate in a live class in Maui that focused on cash flow and velocity banking. Many of us showed up at the bank the next morning to apply what we just learned. I was terrified. I was so afraid of losing all my money. I'm at the credit union opening up a line of credit with my own money, that's how bad my credit was. This was the same credit union that rejected my line of credit application five months prior. This was my

only option at the time. I was praying that this info was correct and that it worked – and it worked for Me! It was nearly all the money I had. It is easier to walk through your fear when someone is sitting right next to you encouraging you all along the way. So, find successful people actively doing the type of real estate deals you want to do. Hang on to their coat tails, so to speak. Learn for them until you build the know-how and confidence to get the right information and then do real estate with confidence in yourself.

Shannon:

When you began your real estate investing career, how important was it for you to establish your team?

Michele:

It was very important. We are in the process of establishing a real estate team of professionals. However, it is very important to grow our community with local team members here in Maui. We're growing our local community, right now. It's amazing and exciting to see new team members join our community each week. These new members bring their own talents and personalities to the community. We are in a rapid growth spurt. There is strength in numbers and our numbers are growing faster than ever right now.

Shannon:

In your business with growing your team, how do you help people learn more about real estate?

Michele:

It depends on what they want to learn more about. We always point them back to the information that's in the education that we have access to. We want to create an environment where we are 'system depend' instead of 'people Depend.' Most times the answers are in the education. We are here to guide and direct them. We found that it's best to plug people into the system and the different local events that we have. It's a good thing to have people experience our local community and the support from other team members.

We hold a Velocity Banking Game night for people interested in learning how to rapidly pay down debt without getting a second job, making extra payments, or skimping on their lifestyle. The velocity banking game is a game exclusive to our organization. It is a fun and interactive type of game that sometimes can get competitive depending on who is playing that night.

It's fascinating to see the 'light bulb' go on as their eyes light up when they realize how much cash flow they end up with at the end of the game. It's a game changer.

Shannon:
What is cash flow and why is it so important?

Michele:
Cash flow is what's left over after all the expenses (mortgage, taxes, insurance etc.) are paid. What's left over is the positive cash flow.

Cash flow is the Holy Grail of real estate and business. Cash flow is the lifeline of a real estate business. Cash flow is the business behind the business. It's the name of the game. Increasing cash flow enables a greater ability to replace earned income from a job. Cash flow is important because without positive cash flow there will be no cash flowing in to feed our families, buy clothes for our children, or put gas in our cars.

Shannon:
What do you think is the number mistake an individual makes when buying their first investment property?

Michele:
Not beginning with the end in mind and not doing their due diligence, or properly analyzing the property, knowing what they are getting into, knowing what to expect, running the numbers, having the proper expectations. And also, buying more than they should—being over leveraged. That is to say, spending more money than their budget can handle. First-time investors many times get excited and jump in, buying impulsively without knowing what they're getting into, without doing proper analysis or running the numbers and having three concrete ways to get out of a deal.

Shannon:
Do you believe that real estate investing success is dependent on a strong economy?

Michele:

No, I don't. We've been taught different strategies. There are different strategies for different markets. This is where good solid current information found in our tool box comes in handy. Knowing what to do, when to do it, and where to do it matters. In the local market where, Maui, Hawaii, the purchase price for property tends to be high all year round. For this reason, many local community members find properties out of state in the mainland when they first begin investing.

Shannon:

How does real estate allow you to make massive or passive income?

Michele:

It all depends on your goals. Passive Income can come from buying property that generates rental income from tenants. Massive Income can come from a combination of ways such as commercial, multi-family, or apartment complex transactions. Buying real estate with your retirement account and using other people's money to purchase property are other ways. Getting into debt using other people's money is very common among wealthy people. In fact, many wealthy people have used debt to acquire their wealth, their massive income. Bottom line is, using other people's money, using debt the right way and using the right tools, can create both passive and massive income all at the same time.

Shannon:

What are some creative ways to acquire a property?

Michele:

One creative way of buying a property is the 'Subject To.' You can buy property subject to the mortgage being paid, or Back taxes being paid, or subject to an inspection being done. This can be whatever conditions you decide on that meet your criteria. There's Seller Financing, the seller will basically become the bank and you make your payments to the seller until the property's paid off or whatever the terms are agreed upon. There's also Lease Option, Contract for Deed, and many other creative ways to acquire properties.

Shannon:
If you were at a family reunion, and somebody looked at you and said, 'how has real estate changed your life' what would you say?

Michele:
It changed my life immensely. I have a totally different mindset when it comes to money, credit, real estate, and resources. I have a better understanding of how money flows and how the wealthy 2% in this country thinks and why. I understand why the wealthy do what they do, their mind set, their way of thinking.

I understand credit from a banker's point of view and as a consumer. I know the five factors that affect my credit score. When I'm making a credit decision that means I will pay down debt and credit cards, shortly after my score will increase. Conversely, sometimes when I am making a financial decision my credit score will decrease temporarily. Therefore, my credit score is constantly changing.

I comprehend real estate markets better now. I comprehend how to analyze a property and its particular market. I understand that the pretty purple-painted bedroom walls don't make the property a good deal or a bad deal. Bottom line: buy by the numbers. If the numbers make sense, make money, bring in the right amount of money, the deals are done.

I know where to look to find properties, and I know how to find properties before they hit the market. I know how to find people with money, with homes free and clear, and absentee owners. I didn't know any of this information before learning about real estate.

I know about finding the money, the resources; most people do not do deals because of the lack of money. They don't have the money; they can't find the money, and they think they need their own money. There's not a shortage of money. Money is all around us. Money is in abundance though there may be a shortage of money in our bank accounts. There is no shortage of access to money either. There is perhaps a lack knowledge, the lack of knowing how and where to access money and resources.

I am a lifelong learner, and I have learned there are several little-known banking tools. There is a difference big between a Line of Credit and a Loan. Knowing this difference has saved me thousands of dollars in interest already.

What I'm working on now is improving my personal credit, using velocity banking to pay down my debt. I am doing my budget, cash flow, banking, and lowering my taxes. Also, I will be working on establishing my business credit which is totally different from my personal credit. The biggest thing I am learning is that I am developing my ability to expand my means. I'm not just living below my means by skimping, saving, and bag lunches to work. I'm developing skills to expand my means, drawing from my credit, and enjoying more tax deductions. What I'm learning was only available to a small group of privileged people up until now.

Shannon:
What type of legacy do you want to leave?

Michele:
I want to leave a legacy of Faith, Hope, Love, Joy, and what I call Total Life Prosperity. Total Life Prosperity means to be prosperous and have an abundance in your character, integrity, keeping your word, being accountable, and being prosperous with Faith and Money. This is the best legacy I can leave to my children. I want them to know that they have the seeds of greatness within them. We are here on this earth to do something great. We are to be the light that most people aren't. If they are consistent and persistent with their actions, and have a burning desire, then they can achieve anything they set their hearts to. We are to have a positive impact on people. We need to find a group, a cause, or a purpose that is higher than they are. We all need something to believe in. The most important thing is FAITH. Faith in God, Faith in yourself, and Faith in something greater than we are; Faith for a cause or a purpose, a place to belong, a place to hang your hat, and be welcomed with open arms.

This is the same legacy I want to be known for when I leave this life. My goal is to leave a legacy to my community where I live, and hopefully this legacy will spread around the world. Also, being prosperous with my time, having an abundance of friends, faith, joy, love, happiness, and money.

We just had a couple of deaths at my job within the last year. People can live their life any way they want to live. However, many of them party, drink excessively, play around with recreational drugs, and are promiscuous. I believe so many people are hurting inside. They are lonely, have lost hope, and have given up on their dreams of a good life. They are discouraged and perhaps feel unsupported. They need to belong to something good.

It's important that people have a hope, a dream, and a future. I know this business can assist and help people in so many areas of life. It can give people a place to belong, a hope in a cause greater than themselves, a chance to rekindle their dreams and create a bright future to look forward to. That's my goal, that's my heart of hearts is to give people hope, a dream, and a future; so, they don't have to lose their lives to drugs, alcohol and depression. My heart of hearts desire is to see the sparkle return to people - knowing that they have a hope for a better and brighter future and something amazing to look forward to every day.

Scott Fredricey

Scott Fredricey had a rural life growing up. His fascination for building things began on the farm at a young age, starting with a chicken coop before the age of 12. That was the beginning of his building career, and the start of his entrepreneurial side. Yes, having so many chickens meant an abundance of eggs. So what else do you when you have that many chickens? He sold the eggs to his teachers and school mates.

Scott continued his education, receiving a BS degree in biology. He had a strong fascination for the water that took him from the Rockies and Colorado plains to California. There, he furthered his education to be a deep-sea diver. But realizing the extreme dangers, as well knowing someone else was in control of your life, led to him switching to high technology, millimeter wave componentry. It was a strong interest and early in his career it paid well, but it was inside work all the time and it became a 9 to 5 JOB.

Meanwhile, to help pay the mortgage and raise two boys, he decided to get back into something that was more familiar – building! His past building experience made it easy for him to get into the trades once again, yet it was still a 9 to 5 JOB. Then he became a contractor in the state of California, and in 2000 SF construction was formed. In the beginning, he was primarily doing residential small repair jobs and bathroom remodels. SF construction had contracts with five Home Depots and one Lowe's in the Santa Barbara Ventura County area of California, and he had placed second and third out of 6000 installers for customer service 4 years in a row.

Then, as SF construction became more commercial as a specialized door Installer, he was back to the 9 to 5. When his team began working on hospitals, schools, and retirement homes, his fascination with commercial real estate grew. He realized the importance of constantly learning about real estate. As he says, that's step one! Implementation and action make up step two.

So for Scott, education is continuing—it is for his lifetime. He believes in updating his education as needed as real estate is always changing. Today Scott is continuing his education to further put his company where it needs to be to operate safely and strongly.

Shannon:

According to Forbes magazine, real estate is one of the top three ways people become wealthy. As a real estate expert, why do you feel this is the case?

Scott:

Well there are many situations in real estate where you don't necessarily need your own money to acquire property, or you don't even have a really good credit score. With the combination of those two it makes it more likely you can put yourself into a stronger financial position using other people's money. That is if you work with the most advanced educated system, you will be far ahead in the real estate realm and less likely to fail. Most people feel they can't do real estate because of the high dollar value! Nothing could be further from the truth. Sure, money helps, but there are many investors that have started with a little and have built small empires.

Shannon:

What inspired you to get into real estate?

Scott:

As a contractor, I've always been fascinated with building things. Growing up on a farm I built a chicken coop when I was 12 years old by myself which housed a hundred chickens plus. I've always been a carpenter. I guess I just have a fascination for putting a shelter overhead, which is one of our essential needs to survive. It has always been my drive to do good for people. So real estate investing just fell right into my lap, especially doing the fix and flips or buy and holds, which usually require some sort of contracting. But there are those homes that do not need much work to turn them around and put him back on the market.

Shannon:

How important was it for you to establish a team when you began your real estate investing?

Scott:

I'm constantly establishing a team, so that is never a task! Having support where someone can bounce ideas off of is important! Talking to your team is very important!

Shannon:
Do you feel like people can be successful in real estate on their own?

Scott:
Well, no. Bottom line is no. You can give it the best effort that you can but most people, even though they claim they're an overnight success or a self-made millionaire, most of them had some backing, support, or direction somewhere along the lines to help them achieve their goals.

Shannon:
How have mentors in your real estate investing helped you navigate potential pitfalls?

Scott:
Using my affiliates to help answer questions has put me in the right place where I need to be at the right time.

Shannon:
In your business, how do you help other people learn more about real estate?

Scott:
I think for me it would be leading by example, so I need to experience and actually do the hands on, whether it's just the reading and gaining the knowledge or the physical aspect of going out and doing door knocking.

Shannon:
How has your education in real estate changed the way that you invest?

Scott:
Well, I look at the numbers more than anything. I guess that's the number one thing its taught me—how to look at the numbers and go about it more wisely in doing my due diligence, like making sure that if there's a downturn in the economy, that I have myself covered.

Shannon:
If you're starting with little money or poor credit, what are some strategies to get into real estate?

Scott:

I feel the most common one would be they call it a 'subject to.' That would be one of the best and easiest strategies used with pre-foreclosures.

Shannon:

Explain to me what a subject to is in your opinion.

Scott:

It is knowing how to use the numbers related to the property value. This is to help the person or persons out of their bad situation which they may be in. That is what we as investors do when some undisclosed undesirables come up; if we find that it's not the ideal project, it gives us a way to exit the contract, but it allows us to, if it works, create a win-win situation for the sellers and the buyers.

Shannon:

You know you've referred to the numbers several times. What are the numbers?

Scott:

The numbers are the relationship of what they owe on their home and what we can acquire the property for related to the market value. It varies from project to project, location to location. If there a second to third loan on the property, all of these financial obligations to the property apply. All this needs to be worked into the negotiation of the purchase of the property. So, working the numbers relates to dollars spent and to the dollars earned.

Shannon:

What are some creative ways that you find these properties?

Scott:

I'm currently in one now that I just drove by it and told myself, 'well that looks like an ideal property.' Because of its situation it's somewhat dilapidated, but at the same time it's semi-occupied. Then I told myself, 'Oh, I should look at that place.' So, I did. I guess it's not really creative but it's something that is still used. It's just drive-by and that's been working for me because of the community I live in is not that large, it makes it easier to cover the territory.

Shannon:

When you do a drive-by and you notice a property like that, what's your next step? How do you find out if that property is actually in distress or if their lawnmower is broken?

Scott:

There are other signs besides just the lawn that give indication that it's in distress. Like maybe the current property has a patchwork roof. Meaning they haven't had the money to fix the roof correctly, but they had it repaired many times. And YES, it does looks like a patch work quilt on their roof.

As a contractor, it's easier for me to spot those distress signs. The roof is just really bold. The first step I did was start asking questions of the tenants that live there to find out what they knew. I found out one of the renters Is putting it up for sale. He used to have control of the deed but didn't make his payments and was foreclosed on and was putting it up for sale. And, ironically, I had to go out of town and then when I came back, there was a for sale sign up on the property. And to me it said good value.

I called the number, telling myself I had to put this into action to make it work because if I would have never called, it would have never happened. In this particular property, the person that I contacted acted as if he was the owner, but he was just a renter who had lost it under foreclosure to the original owner who now controlled the deed again. And the renter I first talked to was renting because he couldn't come up with the money, so the owner foreclosed on him. But the renter still needed the space.

I asked the renter, for the owner's number, and he gave it to me. I called him up and, at the beginning of the conversation, found out that he's also an investor in real estate. He is a hard money lender. So, low and behold I said, 'Perfect, so am I' and suggested we work out a win-win deal. After I gave him my background and history, he was pretty excited to have someone take control of the property who cares.

He was going to go back to the renter because he had come up with his payment but didn't want to give him a third chance. Since I came along, he said he would give me a try and here we are in escrow. There was a little snafu due to a lien on the property, but the paperwork wasn't finalized until after payment. I refused to sign any further papers until all that was taken care of in escrow office.

Isn't the quickest way to get things done where I live, but they're pretty efficient, which is the most important part.

Shannon:
You made mention of the tenant being in foreclosure.

Scott:
Right, well currently he is not as he stayed on the property as a renter. He was foreclosed on and then the original owner took the property back. But the renter I originally talked to put up the for-sale sign. And what's ironic here is what the education teaches you. As a renter, you don't start sinking your money into a property, but that's what he did. As a renter he started putting money into it, then renting the spaces out. This process is totally backwards.

Shannon:
He could really use some education, couldn't he?

Scott:
Absolutely. At some point I will present him with the proper education. He would really benefit from the array of education within the system! I told him he can continue to rent the barn and put as much of his stuff in it as needed to get it out of the units, so we can repair them and get them rented out ASAP. He can continue to rent a little space from me for a while.

I am creating a win-win for him too, even though he's not the owner. I will show him how to go in the right direction.

All the renters are going to be able to stay in the place, but within 90 days there will be a rent adjustment because the rent is lowest in town. And I can't have that because we are doing the highest quality of work on the property. The rent will ease up to a low rate but not necessarily the lowest rate in town.

Shannon:
Speaking of rates, what is cash flow and why should it be such an important focus of your business?

Scott:
This particular property already has a positive cash flow. That positive cash flow will enable my business to improve the property with-

out it costing the business money. Then once those projects are done, I will be able to have that going into my pocket as opposed to into the property.

I will always put a certain amount aside for the property, but then the majority of it will be going to my pocket.

Shannon:

Do you feel that real estate investing success is dependent on a strong economy?

Scott:

No. No, not at all. There are several factors to take into consideration. When the economy is in a downturn, investing is on an upswing. You have to be a lot more cautious and not overpay for a property. But that's actually one of the most beneficial times for a real estate investor because properties become way more affordable. But of course, there are other factors besides the economy, like divorce, death in the family, and so on. These things never stop happening!

Shannon:

What advice would you give to someone who is allowing fear to hold them back from starting their real estate investing?

Scott:

I have a lot of fears. The fear of the unknown and I guess some fear of rejection. Because as a successful contractor going into a new realm of the same field, I have certain fears of approaching people that are in distress. But I found that they really want your help.

And the first property where I have just relocated too will be mine as soon as escrow closes. I found out a lot of things about this new community by asking questions and doing. I already found how easy people are to work with if you're proactive in making sure that their concerns and qualifications are all met. When you do that, it's not a nightmare like people think it is. Which helps drive away the fear. People want to be helped, especially when they are in a bad situation financially.

Sure, there are certain challenges, but you know you just have to face it and once you face it, you realize that there's always a solution, easing the fear.

Shannon:
How does real estate allow you to earn massive and passive income?

Scott:
Passive is a general term. You know in passive income there's always something a little involved that you have to do. Maybe you have to talk with a property management company that handles the property, but there's still always something to do. Passive income is I feel too loose of a term, but it is the least binding because it's money that is positive into your account without you doing any further work.

There's just deal after deal after deal. It's getting a little bit more challenging because as more and more people become educated, they get out there into other areas where they never thought they would. More and more people are getting into it, but there's just so much real estate out there it would be hard for all the real estate investors to overtake it.

You have your realtors that list on the MLS too, and that's a whole other field of real estate. As investors get involved with that too, but we don't look it as a commission. We look at as a win-win situation for the previous owner and ourselves, no commission. Occasionally as you know we work with realtors, they are paid a commission, so they are getting a smaller lump sum as to what an investor would be making.

Shannon:
If someone wanted to invest in multi-family dwellings, what do they need to know?

Scott:
It's just more involved, it is almost the same thing as a single location but more of it. You know when you do multi-dwelling as the property investor, the numbers are still negotiated; it is all real estate. In conventional real estate, commercial properties are a little bit more expensive to purchase because you need a minimum of 40 to 50 percent down. That's not the case in investing! It is still the terms that you and the previous owner negotiate for that acquisition of the property. Commercial property may be one large structure or several small structures or a combination of structures. One thing with commercial property is there's more living space per square foot of land. As an example: the one piece of property I deal with has 12 toilets, so I have

12 of everything, not just one. The cost of commercial property can add up very quickly.

One thing to take into consideration will it be a fix and flip, or buy and hold, or do a lease option. In my case I am doing a buy and hold. Although if I sell this particular property, the note becomes due immediately. The owner is carrying the balance for three years with one point with no payments, due to the amount of work that needs to be done on the property.

With commercial you might get a storefront with some apartments. It all depends on what you're looking for and how much effort you want to put into it.

If you want to do it as a buy and hold, which is a more long-term strategy, then you need the capital to be able to do those improvements. Since the property that I have needs some improvements and it already has a positive cash flow, then I can start slowly doing some of the improvements.

The improvements to be completed are the ones that are the easiest units to fix and get rented out to create more passive cash flow!

Shannon:
Most millionaires and billionaires have investments in commercial real estate. Why do you think this is the case?

Scott:
Well you get more revenue per square foot of land, so like in my case the property that I'm in escrow with is commercial property. It has already some units on it which take up less space. With just a little alteration to the commercial rating I will be able to put more units on it or RV overnight parking. This is a pretty inexpensive proposition, and by doing my due diligence I found out in talking with the city assessor that I can set up some RV parking as long as I meet their regulations, which is pretty easy for me to do as a contractor.

One more thing, we covered this a little bit with residential in regard to subject to. Even this commercial property that I'm in, it's not really a subject to. Although I do have an exit clause! I'm doing a buy and hold strategy. I guess it could be subject to because if they disclose that the lien that was supposed to be paid off wasn't paid off and it's a substantial amount, I have a clause in there that I will be able to exit the contract, that's really important.

Shannon:

Why is it so important to have that clause in there? What would be the repercussion if that lien was not paid off?

Scott:

Everybody that I talked to said that there were no judgments against the property, meaning no liens. If there was a lien and say it was $40,000, well that wouldn't make it affordable now unless we renegotiated some terms. It might make it not worth the deal and you could exit. Because now there's more money that is on the table that shouldn't have been there according to if someone was telling the truth when they said everything was paid off. Yes, people don't always tell the truth about their property in financial situations!

And supposedly everything was paid off and they dropped the ball in completing the payoff paper work that stated that it was paid off. If it wasn't paid off, there's an exit clause!

I won't close unless I know all that information is in order because I don't want to have to deal with another $40,000 on a property that's distressed. It's already enough work without having to pay for their expenses.

Shannon:

What type of legacy do you want to leave?

Scott:

Well in showing my two sons and my granddaughter how to put into action, and not just talk about, what you've learned. You put into action the things that you can achieve. And as for them, both my sons are in a good life direction, but they're going to realize how easy it can be to be even more successful if you have the right education.

It's not without its work though, as you know. I should say it's easier though. There's nothing easy in life. I mean you'd have to put forth the effort to actually do it.

John & Karen Gill

John Gill worked 25 years in aviation and aerospace while his wife Karen did procurement for the USPS until they both got the idea of moving out of the city into a rural part of the state. They bought some acreage in southern Arizona and built a house, meant to be their for-ever-home, a place to create memories and a harbor for their four grown children and five grandchildren. Along with this dream they wanted to start a small business of some kind but were not sure what it would be. Having settled into new local jobs, Karen with the post office and John now working for general contractors, the dream of a small business was never pursued. In 2015 they were presented an opportunity that re-ignited the idea of small business; it was a unique educational product and a community of real estate investors with whom they could begin to network while learning. This was a perfect way for John and Karen to work together and allow their skill sets to complement each other's. So, another new journey was underway for them. Their first real estate deal out-performed John's W2 annual wages, so they were all-in for real estate at that point. John left his W2 job in April of 2017 and Karen retired after 22 years of service in July of 2017, having become full-time real estate professionals. They currently own commercial property that cash flows and also flip houses, which is generating funds to acquire more rentals, both resi-dential and commercial.

Shannon:

According to Forbes magazine, real estate is one of the top three ways people become wealthy. As a real estate expert, why do you feel this is the case?

John:

There are many different ways that I can affect the value of real estate, and the range of price fluctuations with these assets is awesome. Since there are many ways we can make money with them, if you learn what to do and when to do it, and you know your market, you can position yourself well. The wealth is there for the taking—there is no shortage of real estate.

Shannon:

What inspired you personally to get into real estate?

John:

I was nearing retirement age and figured I had about 10 more years that I could work, but I really didn't have a very good pension. My 401(k) had been dissolved in the 1990s, by negligence and the stock market turning around—it all disappeared. Having seen a family member do very well with real estate, I believed I could do the same. The speed with which we can create wealth and a retirement income through passive income was my inspiration.

Shannon:

Karen, do you have anything you'd like to add to that?

Karen:

Yes. Real estate, and people making money off of real estate, has been going on through all the centuries. So, it's been a proven fact. When you look at the wealthy 1 percent like you said, 74 percent of them are small business owners, real estate entrepreneurs. When we got into our education we understood that we were in the W2 99 percent category, and when we saw what the 1 percent wealthy were doing it was a real eye opener for us, as John stated. We were ending our careers soon, having pensions and social security, but that was all we were looking to live on. But now we see that we can make a difference in our lives, in our friends' lives, and in other people's lives.

The idea of real estate has really opened up so many opportunities for our family and learning how to leave legacy wealth.

Shannon:
How does real estate allow you to learn massive and passive income?

John:
Well we have been flipping houses to produce massive income for our capital. We also have some commercial buy & hold suites providing passive income. We made $130,000 in profits on our last two deals. That gave us some breathing room. So, I have the ability to manage the rentals and to do some sweat equity on these fix and flips; it's a good fit for us, that strategy. We're new into buy & holds so we are actually getting our third commercial suite ready to rent out right now.

Shannon:
What is cash flow and why is it important to your business?

John:
Cash flow is one of the fruits of our labor; in real estate, it is the seed for growth. It's important to our business for growth and stability. We want to get out of the flipping business in the future and allow the cash flow from free-and-clear assets to provide personal income and fund our family trust; cash flow is the key to this business model's success.

Karen:
Cash flow is a very important necessity learned from our education. With a lot of people, it doesn't matter what they make, just so the bills are paid. They have the same coming in as they do going out. They aren't concerned enough that they are not getting anywhere. They aren't growing, and they aren't producing. Many people have become complacent, but there are people who want more. I can help the people who want more. They must understand that in a budget or for asset accumulation, cash flow is the key to breaking the poverty cycle. Cash flow is very important to us and we now have employed velocity banking to help increase that cash flow. Currently we've been building up our capital and then we are going to do more buy and holds. Cash flow and I are good friends!

Shannon:

If someone was going to get started in real estate, what you would recommend they do first?

John:

Begin with some education and never stop learning. Discover who you are in the real estate world and what your strengths and aptitudes are. Everyone has different talents, dynamic, and intellect. Do what appeals to you—it should be enjoyable. Then structure your entities with tax and legal considerations before you really do anything. There's about 30 different strategies with real estate, so what you choose depends on the person, but I think the common thread everyone should concern themselves with is gaining knowledge and the business aspects of your ventures. Have enthusiasm and patience.

Karen:

You need to have a vision, you need to have a mission, and you have to be able to set goals. This will give you a high probability of executing those short-term and long-term goals for success.

Shannon:

In your business, how do you help other people learn more about real estate?

John:

We host opportunity presentations for local and national real estate investor communities. We'll host seminars and do live training events; we have weekly meetings, biweekly meetings, and give property tours. We also mentor new investors and possibly partner with people in real estate deals. We're always available to our network and our local community.

Karen:

Our leadership team implemented a 'game night' playing cash flow to introduce people to real estate investing where they can practice real estate investing strategies using play money. You can watch them have their epiphany—the light bulb comes on—they are starting to see the process. Their belief system changes, and they are now inspired to learn more and have gained the confidence to do so.

Shannon:
How have mentors in your real estate investing helped you to navigate potential pitfalls?

Karen:
The pitfalls to real estate investing weren't learned through mentorship as much as what we learned in our education that had specific classes regarding pitfalls. Although the large community serves in many ways as a mentor and a much broader base of knowledge is available.

Shannon:
What advice would you give to someone who is allowing fear to hold them back from starting their real estate investing?

John:
Well, fear will never go away until you confront it. So, we always recommend that people set achievable short-term goals that are part of an overall plan; have a clear objective of what it is that you want to do. In this way you can approach the fearful thing and gain confidence in yourself as you execute the short-term goal. Set your long-term goals higher than your obstacles; don't let fear of these obstacles or discouragement keep you from making any attempt. See the prize and start to think big instead of thinking small. Fear can be confronted, and we can mitigate the risk by getting an education and networking with our real estate community.

Karen:
To quote Bob Newhart, "It's really simple, just two little words . . . STOP IT!" When we were W2 wage-earners, we were in jobs that were competitive, and when we got involved with the education and the team, we learned that these people were collaborative. There is a big difference between competitive and collaborative. Working with a community of collaborative people has created a fearless environment for me. Shift your focus to solutions rather than problems.

Shannon:
Do you feel that real estate investing success is dependent on a strong economy?

John:

No, not at all. There are many different strategies that work depending on what the market's doing and what the economy is doing, so you just have to be able to shift gears and know when to do what. Since we are controlling assets you really just use them differently; learn what the strategies are and how to employ them.

Karen:

I agree with John; if you know the ebbs and flows of the economy and the different strategies that go along with those ebbs and flows, then you don't worry about those things. It's just a matter of a decision of what you are going to implement now: 'what's the next thing we're going to implement?' So, when you have the knowledge, there's no fear factor and worries about the economy. In fact, there will be an abundance of opportunities in a downturned economy, just of a different kind.

Shannon:

How has your education in real estate changed the way that you invest?

John:

That's a good question. It's completely changed the way I invest. We used to invest through savings and planned for scarcity while letting other people manage our money. Now, we manage the money ourselves, we think much bigger. We've taken our money back from the investments where we had it and used it to leverage real estate deals. We're experiencing gains of 50 percent-100 percent versus 1 percent to 2 percent in the stock market—or even less than that in the bank. We've also learned to take our cash flow and use it for growth.

Karen:

I have learned how to take many tax deductions by setting up small businesses. I LOVED learning that I could implement better investment strategies by taking away control from the banks and manage my own investments. Now I make money with the bank's money rather than the bank making money with my money. I am using the knowledge of leveraging my money using credit lines, i.e., HELOCs, and using simple interest versus amortized.

Shannon:
What is one of the top real estate strategies that you have learned?

John:
I think the top ones for us, the ones that we have used and employed, are flipping houses and just doing buy & holds. A lot of people start with those because they are relatively simple, there's not a lot of risk, and there's a lot of income to be made. We have a lot of strategies to learn though. I see many commercial opportunities for cash flow and multi-family too. Cash flow is always good in any form. It's manageable and you can do it on a small scale or as big as you want to get. You can start with one or two rental properties; you can get a duplex, four-plex, something like that. Start to create cash flow. We started where a lot of people did with flipping and buy & holds.

Karen:
This is what we do: when we're buying, of course we buy low and sell high, but it's really about working with people. When they're selling their home, they're hoping to get what they want. You usually have to educate them on what their house is really worth because people are in love with their house, and the sentimentality attached to it kind-of blinds them to what the value really is. But when you can educate them and show them what the property's worth, then you end up really helping them out, and they end up thanking you for taking the house off their hands. Still, the numbers are there for you so that you know you are going to make your profit. My top strategy is to make it a win-win for everybody.

Shannon:
Do you guys have a favorite acquisition strategy?

John:
We tend to just look at the local market, try and catch stuff before it hits the market or before it goes to auction. There is an abundance of distressed properties, but we discriminate. We want something that will sell easily. We like the hunt—homes on the MLS that won't sell. We find out why and see if we can make a deal for both parties.

Karen:

Though we haven't done a 'subject to' yet, I would love to begin to acquire some subject to properties for our portfolio.

Shannon:

If someone wanted to invest in multifamily dwellings, what do they need to know? Think of it this way. What's different in a multifamily than in a single family?

Karen:

Well, the town we live in has an army base, so we have a lot of veterans and active-duty who have access to VA benefits, so we are helping them to understand how to use their VA benefits to acquire a four-plex multi-family dwelling. Living in one of them and renting out three of them can produce cash-flow. A lot of young adults are learning that they can have these assets all lined up for their future. They can support themselves and their families when they get out. Everybody, I believe, does graduate to multi-family. Although we have our little niche now, that doesn't mean that we don't plan on expanding into these larger areas in the future. It's nice owning four or more properties under one roof.

John:

I like multi-family. I've actually looked at many of them over the last year, but we haven't acquired one. What concerns me the most, as I would advise someone, is to consider the structure and configuration. For example, a friend of mine just sold his. It was a 10-unit apartment complex, but every unit was a single structure. It was an old WWII military housing complex that had gone civil. During the cost analysis, there was so much more exterior wall to maintain and so much more roof line to take care of. You have too many exterior doors and storage rooms and all kinds of separate parking arrangements and fences. It had virtually no common walls or outdoor spaces. The maintenance costs would have been very high. If you had a larger building that had ten units under one roof and one parking lot/driveway, a common trash location, common sewer, playground, etc., this would be a better investment according to my numbers. A multi-family investment should always give you cash flow; renovations and evictions can be made on a per-unit basis. With single-family, you can experience long periods of time with no revenue at all depending on the tenants the property needs or evictions.

Shannon:
When doing a short sale, what should you anticipate?

Karen:
We haven't done a short-sale yet, but I know you need to be patient because it's a lengthy process. You should anticipate having many documents in a process with many steps. You'll have to be the facilitator to push the sale through. I advise that you have good people skills.

Shannon:
How are you guys creating win-win situations?

Karen:
We can create win-win situations by helping distressed sellers to identify their needs and understand the complexity of the situations they are in. We show them where they are on a timeline, give them a better understanding of their options, educate them on the true value of their home, the rehab costs, and the current market value. Now a deal can be made that is beneficial to both parties. Another win is for the buyer: they get a beautiful remodeled home they just absolutely love; our houses sell quickly. We average 13 days on market. This means the neighborhood, city, and school districts win too. On a side note, we help our community when we put our subcontractors to work. And everything that we buy locally for renovations are helping the economy. We believe that every company should have some sort of charity that they give to—ours are local.

Shannon:
How has real estate investing changed your life?

John:
Real estate has changed my life in a significant way. I get to do what I like to do. I'm a builder so I am a very hands-on type of person. Now I get to do things my own way; what I want to do and when I want to do it. I get to make more money doing it—much more than I did before. We own the properties; I love the commercial buildings that we're working on right now. I love that fact that we're going to be holding

these for years to come so it gives me a place to teach my grandkids. We have our own business in one of the suites and lease out the other two. Increasing its cash flow and value—that's my job.

Karen:
Well, unlike working at the post office, I now have an office building of my own. In September, I am going to go for my real estate license and open a real estate agency in my commercial building. Then, I am going to be earning those commissions that I'm paying out to realtors currently. I really like that I'm my own boss, and like John says, we love what we do, and we love working together. We complement each other not only in life but also in our business and our talents. My life has changed because real estate has allowed me to pursue a dream of being a business owner.

Shannon:
Final question, what is the legacy that you would like to leave behind?

Karen:
The legacy that I would like to leave behind is something that wasn't taught in high school. What I would like to do is create a scholarship fund for high school students to get a specialized education in real estate investing. I would also like to see something that really helps not only the individuals in our family but also our community with the way we set up our trust.

John:
I would like to have cash flowing assets that will fund a living trust of some kind to function as a family bank. From that trust, we could continue to fund charities and provide our children and grand-children opportunities to use these funds for their own ventures after we are gone. We want to help improve the lives of people in our community and help our church with projects and growth. We can leave assets that will fund things like this. I think that would be a nice legacy to leave behind and it would live on. I hope the success doesn't stop. We'd like to teach this to some of our family members—our grandchildren probably—so that they can continue doing the same thing because if it all stops somewhere then you really haven't been successful.

Jeff & Janet Grenier

Jeff and Janet Grenier have been entrepreneurs for over 25 years. Jeff, a former truck driver, was always looking for a better way to provide for his family. Growing up in an entrepreneurial family he was always seeking business opportunities. Looking for something to work for them, Jeff and Janet have owned many businesses, including brick and mortar, online, and work-from-home companies. In January of 2015, they finally found what they were looking for: a business opportunity that provides education and is attached to a community.

Through that education system and the community, they now enjoy living a life of financial freedom and helping others get out of the rat race. Their current passion is real estate investing and helping others seek out their path to financial literacy. They do share this unique opportunity with as many people as they can in the hopes of creating a better world now and for future generations.

Jeff and Janet have been happily married for 26 years. They live in Plainfield, Illinois, with their sons, Matthew and Jonathan, and their dog, Wylie. They enjoy spending time with family and friends, meeting new people, going for rides on Jeff's Harley, and traveling abroad. They are committed to helping people better their lives and fulfilling not only their dreams and aspirations but helping others achieve the same.

Shannon:

According to Forbes magazine, real estate is one of the top three ways that people become wealthy. As real estate experts, why do you feel this is the case?

Jeff:

I feel that real estate is one of the best ways to create wealth because people will always need a place to live. There are so many advantages to investing in real estate. We make money doing fix and flips; we take a property that has been neglected and add value. In the rental market, even when the market crashed in '08, rents stayed where they were, and in some areas rents elevated due to demand. If the value of the property decreases, the tenants can't ask for a rent reduction. You have tenants in your properties paying the mortgage, taxes, maintenance, repairs etc. The tenants pay all the expenses, and the owner gets all the tax write-offs, appreciation, and cash flow.

Shannon:

What inspired you personally to get into real estate?

Jeff:

Okay, so for me, one of the reasons we got into it is because we ran into some really hard times in our life with a few different things. We got to the point where we were living check to check, and we found we had a lot more month than money. We were looking for a way to get out of debt. I was looking for a way to improve our marriage as well because when there is such a lack of money in your life that you don't have even enough for necessities, it tends to cause a little friction in the marriage. I saw an opportunity, through a community of investors, to change our situation.

One of the things I found out since we've become successful in investing in real estate and money is coming in, is that hardship has gone away.

Shannon:

Janet, how has real estate changed your life?

Janet:

It has changed my life on so many different levels. The education has broadened my mind and the people from the community are a constant source of support and wisdom. Neither of us are the same people we were three years ago. We've become better versions of ourselves and are constantly changing and improving. I never would have thought that one simple decision would spur such remarkable changes in our lives. The life we lead now is a completely different and a completely satisfying life.

Shannon:

In your business, how do you help other people learn more about real estate?

Janet:

We help them by showcasing our online education. If they decide it's something they want to pursue, we become their advisors and guide them on their path. Through this community we actually have learned that by helping other people achieve their goals, in the end we achieve our goals too. It's the complete opposite of climbing the corporate ladder, scratching and clawing your way to the top. In our world now, we reach down to help people up and there's always hands reaching down to help us up. It's pretty amazing.

Shannon:

How has your education in real estate changed the way that you invest?

Jeff:

Oh, it has changed it immensely. In the past, we dabbled in the stock market, but the returns were not enough to create wealth for us. We learned how to become real estate investors through an online education system with practitioner instructors. They do what they teach as their full-time business. They not only teach us applications, they share their successes and their past mistakes, so that we can learn from them. Due to us being part of a local community of investors, we surround ourselves with like-minded, successful people on a weekly basis. We are just a product of the product—we engaged in our education and took action and, most importantly, we applied what we learned.

Shannon:

What is one of the top real estate strategies that you have learned?

Janet:
Well, we've learned so many different real estate strategies. I would say that the top two would be the strategies of fix and flip and buy and holds. We've also learned wholesaling, tax deeds and liens, commercial, multi-units, vacant land...

Jeff:
For me one of the nice things about what I've learned about being a real estate investor is that we're problem solvers. We meet people with issues with their real estate: maybe they're in pre-foreclosure, maybe they are changing jobs, maybe they just have to get out of their house, maybe it's a divorce thing. We've learned that we're problem solvers. We can go in and we can sit down with people and see what their needs are. Because in every case, every real estate deal is different.

We like to meet with the owners of the property, see what their needs are, and see if we can come up with a plan. We give them our offer and give details why our offer is what it is, we try to come up with a plan so both sides see it as a fair deal. We do our best to help solve their problems and we make money doing just that. I love it because when I put my head on the pillow at night, I sleep well because I know that every day we're doing our best to help someone in need.

Shannon:
When you're doing a fix and flip, and you're using that strategy, what is one thing that you want to look out for?

Janet:
Just one thing?

Jeff:
One thing. (laughing) Well, there's a lot of things, but one thing is to make sure that we do our due diligence to make sure that the property is exactly what the seller is telling us it is. Like hiring the right professionals to make sure there is a clean title, no liens on the property, and a good inspector to evaluate the condition of the property and the components. And most importantly to make sure we do our numbers correctly to make sure it is a profitable deal.

Janet:
Right. I'll add to that. Also, make sure that if it doesn't end up being a viable fix and flip, that we have another exit strategy in place that we feel comfortable using, either turning it into a rental or a lease option, because markets change so you have to keep that in mind and be well aware of it.

Shannon:
On that note, when you're looking for a buy and hold, or for something that you know that you want to add to your portfolio as a rental, what are you looking for there?

Jeff:
Cash flow.

Janet:
Definitely cash flow and also that you know the average rent prices in that area for that type of property. Because you don't want to price yourself too high or too low, you want to be right in the median of rentals in that area.

Jeff:
Yeah you'll watch market rents, that's for sure. And you want to make sure that if the property has an association, that the association allows rentals.

Janet:
Yes.

Jeff:
You want to make sure that it's exactly what Janet says, that the rents are market rents that you can actually have cash flow. And the cash flow depends on your needs. I mean, there are people that are happy with a $20 a month cash flow. And there are people that want $500-$600 a month in cash flow. It depends on individual needs.

There's a number of things to consider.

Shannon:
What is cash flow, and why is it so important to your business?

Jeff:
Sure. So, cash flow is the money that is left over after paying the bills. When you have a rental property, you've got to remember that you have to pay taxes, insurance, interest, mortgage, and you want a positive cash flow. Meaning that after all the bills are paid, you've still got money coming in. That's having your maintenance funds set aside and everything, so you're set up. The rents come in, you pay all the bills, and cash flow is what is left over. Basically, cash flow is your profit at the end of the month.

Shannon:
If someone wanted to invest in multi-family dwellings, what do they need to know?

Janet:
For a multi-family it is a completely different system on how to evaluate it. It's not the same as how you evaluate a single family or a property that is four units and below. So it's a completely different formula you use to evaluate it.

Jeff:
It's based on what they call a 'cap rate,' a capitalization rate. A cap rate is based on income versus expenses. One thing that people need to know if they're looking at a multi-family unit is that they have to get exact expenses. They need to see exactly what the expenses are and not just what the seller is telling them they are. Ask the seller for the Schedule E that will show the expenses they paid. But buyer beware because not every seller is honest about the true expenses of a property, this is where due diligence comes in.

Janet:
I would also suggest asking the seller for a profit and loss statement.

Jeff:
Yeah. You need to know what that exactly is, that the numbers jive. And it goes off the cap rate.

Shannon:
How can a real estate investor benefit from notes, tax liens, or deeds?

Jeff:

The notes business is huge. This is when an investor becomes the bank on a deal. Someone buys a note on real property and the note holder gets the monthly payment, principal plus interest. Tax liens are another huge business in that when someone defaults on their property taxes, the county needs to get paid, so an investor can come to an auction and makes the taxes current and become the owner, but they do not take possession yet. There is a redemption period that allows the defaulting party to come current by paying the investor for the taxes plus interest at a rate pre-determined by the county. If they do not pay, the buyer of the tax lien can then take possession of the property. Every county has guidelines in how this process works.

Janet:

Right, as Jeff mentioned, it's based on the county guidelines. All of them are different but it can be a lucrative strategy. If the party in default pays off the taxes, then you get your money back plus interest. If they don't pay off the taxes, then you acquire the property for what you paid for it in the taxes that were due.

Shannon:

How do learning multiple investing strategies protect and accelerate your investing success?

Jeff:

Every single deal is completely different. Again, we are in the problem-solving business. Someone who has a property that either wants out or needs out can come to us with their unique situation, and we have a strategy to help them. The key for us is having multiple different exit strategies. Before we acquire a property, we determine different ways we can exit because you never know what the future may hold. The more strategies you know, the better your chances are of completing deals successfully.

I suggest anybody who wants to get into real estate investing learn as many strategies as they can because you never know what's going to come up for you. Our education covers fix and flips, short sales, lease options, buy and holds, tax deeds and liens, and so much more. So, when people come to us with their situation, we are prepared and educated to help solve their problem. A well-rounded investor knows how to handle any situation that is brought to them.

Janet:
Right and will be much more successful. The more knowledge you have, the more successful you'll be.

Jeff:
And one of the benefits that we have because we're in a real estate investing community is that we learn about these strategies first hand. We're also surrounded by seasoned investors that we can ask questions of who are available if we just want to make sure that we are on the right path. One thing that I learned from hanging out with successful people is that they freely share their knowledge and also are not afraid to ask questions or even ask for help.

Shannon:
Do either of you have a favorite investment strategy?

Jeff:
Actually, the favorite for me right now is fix and flips because we came in here with a lot of debt. And fixing and flipping is nice because you can make enough money that you can actually take care of debts in a fast way. However, you only get paid one time on a fix and flip. My absolute favorite way though, for long-term, is buy and holds.

Janet:
I completely agree. Fix and flips are a terrific way to earn cash fast, but I'm super excited to start building a rental portfolio for monthly cash flow.

Jeff:
Having a building, and having tenants in there who are paying the mortgage, taxes, insurance, maintenance and repairs, plus cash flow—I don't see how it can be any better than that. Here's the nice thing that I love about the rental strategy. It's actually the best way for us to create wealth, and it's a way for us to leave a legacy. Because we can take these properties, and we can will them to our kids or even grandkids. So this is a legacy that we are creating by getting involved in real estate. That's why to me it is the best way in this country to make money and create wealth.

Shannon:

Do either of you have a favorite strategy to acquire a property? Do you have a favorite way that you say, 'okay, we're going to go look for a fix and flip, this is what we're going to do, or we're going to go look for a buy and hold, this is what we're going to do'?

Janet:

I would say being part of the real estate community we're in, it actually benefits us because we get a lot of word-of-mouth referrals from other members of the community. People in our lives outside of the community also know we're investors. If they know of someone who needs help with a property for whatever reason, they will contact us. In my opinion, I like that strategy the best.

Jeff:

And in the community we're involved with, once you start plugging in, you start evolving. For someone who is new to real estate, like we were, will find that there are four stages of real estate investing. For us, we started out wholesaling, then we got into fix and flips, now we're getting into buy and holds, and then eventually we would like to be the money lenders (we can actually be the bank). Right now, we have a lot of ways that we find deals, by the people in the group that are in phase one of their investing career wholesaling deals to us. We also are finding out that people who were in trouble in the past that we've helped are referring others to us. To me that's awesome because while we're doing one deal, we've got people bringing us others so we don't have to spend the time looking for properties. They bring us the deals; they give us the numbers, and then we do our due diligence to make sure the deal meets our criteria.

Shannon:

Most millionaires and billionaires have investments in commercial real estate. Why do you think that is?

Jeff:

I believe it's because the commercial tenants are usually more stable; they are running their business there, and they want to establish a location that they can be at for a long term. They are not looking to move around like a residential tenant may be.

Shannon:
What type of legacy do you want to leave?

Jeff:
I want to be remembered as being a good business person who was very ethical and had a lot of integrity. I want to leave a legacy for generations to come that I was a role model for our community and our kids, our kid's kids, their kids, and so on. That they can get into business for themselves, it doesn't have to be real estate, although I hope that they all do it, but working for yourself will actually get you a lot further than ever working for somebody else. Because I believe when you wake up in the morning, you have two choices: you either get up to build your dreams or somebody else's.

Also, I don't want to speak for Janet, but I think she will agree with me, we want to be known for not only providing well for our family but also for our community and for those who need it. We want to be known for being generous not only with money but our time as well. I always believe in leaving somewhere better than you found it, and I definitely want to be known and remembered as that guy.

Janet:
Yes, that we can show people that they don't have to suffer along in a 9-5 job. If you're willing to put in the work and effort, in the long run you're going to make a better life for yourself, for your children, your family, and for everyone your life touches along the way.

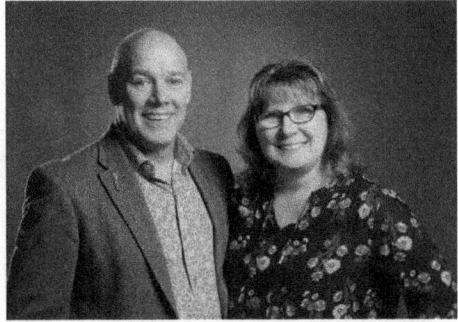

Scott & Allison Huminsky

Scott and Allison Huminsky have been business owners for over 25 years. They currently reside in Shorewood, Illinois, and together they currently run three successful businesses. Their main focus is on growing their rental portfolio to provide constant income for retirement.

They started out with a small business that focused on side jobs for Scott which included small construction projects such as decks, additions, kitchens, windows, siding, garages and more. Scott was a carpenter by trade, so this business was an obvious start for them. Their many years in these projects peaked their interest in real estate investing.

After training with the top real estate education company in the country, they started their second company, ASR Investments Inc., and became full-time real estate investors. In the beginning, the main focus was on fix and flip projects, as that is what Scott knew well. He had built custom homes for the past 20+ years and knew how to manage construction projects from the ground up. Scott took great pride in taking a house that needed serious help and turning it into a beautiful home for a family to enjoy.

Allison had always worked in the customer service industry so her ability to multitask and keep the logistical side of the business running efficiently make them a great team.

They are also passionate about changing lives by raising awareness regarding financial responsibility, debt and interest reduction, tax mitigation, and wealth creation. They are supporters of the Responsibility Foundation and The Statue of Responsibility movement and help raise awareness of this important project.

Today they focus on managing their 33 rental properties and continuing to look for more to add to their portfolio as well as continuing to do fix and flips when the opportunities arise. They are also invested in creating educated real estate investors and creating new income opportunities for like-minded entrepreneurs.

Shannon:

According to Forbes magazine, real estate is one of the top three ways people become wealthy. As a real estate expert, why do you feel this is the case?

Scott:

Real estate is a tangible asset that won't ever go away, unlike the stock market you know, where you could lose the stock, but with real estate the asset is always going to be there. Heaven forbid something happens to it, it's insured, so the insurance policy gives you the value of the asset to replace it. It's as though when purchased properly the asset can never be subject to loss, it might go up and down in value, but it will always be there.

Shannon:

If someone was going to start in real estate what would you recommend they do first?

Scott:

I would say find a group or community of likeminded people that are looking to achieve the same things you are. You can get a lot more done learning with others than on your own.

Shannon:

Allison, in your business how do you help other people learn more about real estate?

Allison:

We listen and learn what their problems are and then show them ways to find the best answer to solve their challenges. With most people there are multiple ways of looking at their situation, so we try to help them find the best possible outcome for their issue.

Shannon:

How about you, Scott? Do you have anything that you'd like to add to that?

Scott:

We introduce them to our community and show them there are hundreds of people just like them who are also looking to change their lives and to find a better way. Most everyone you meet would like to make more money or get out of debt. We just help them to see what it possible by investing in themselves first and real estate second. It is just so hard to try to go out on your own and make money. It seems to be a heck of a lot easier to do it as you are helping others achieve the same goals as you.

Shannon:
What inspired you to get into real estate?

Scott:
Honestly, from being broke. We were at a point where I was currently unemployed, and my daughter asked if she could take ballet lessons. I had to tell her that she couldn't sign up for ballet lessons because daddy didn't have a job, and we couldn't afford it. I knew then that there had to be some way that I could fulfill my own destiny and never be in that situation again, having a W-2 job and relying on employers to give me money for my time.

Shannon:
So, Allison, when Scott came to you and said, 'We're going to get started in real estate investing,' what was your first thought?

Allison:
I was like, 'Go for it.' I knew he had every ounce of smarts to do it. He's been in the construction industry for 20+ years. He knew tons of people that could help him work on the projects. I fully believed in him and was like let's do this, because I knew then this would be an opportunity for me to get out of my job as well. So, I have always been fully supportive of him and everything he does.

Shannon:
If you're starting with very little money or poor credit, what are some strategies that you can use to get into real estate?

Scott:
Well, the first strategy on the list would be wholesaling. That is where you find a property with under-market value and sell it to a rehabber or end buyer still under market but with a fee added in for your services. Another little more advanced strategy would be 'subject to'

deals. This is where you go in and help someone by catching them up on their mortgage and take over their payments. In this way you help them by not getting a foreclosure on their record and, in the meanwhile, help them rebuild their credit and get back on their feet. Not every deal is just about finding the money, there are different sources, you know? There are different values of currency, and money is just one of them. You could partner with somebody that has deal or somebody that does the renovations of the deal or somebody that is good at finding money lenders for the deal. They all could be business partners that could help you with what you're trying to achieve, and you'll gain experience along the way.

Shannon:
When you began your real estate investing career, how important was it to establish a strong team to help you be successful?

Scott:
Oh, it was very important. You can't conquer the world by yourself, so you need a team there to help you. Having others with the same desires, drive, and skill set on your team is invaluable to your levels of success.

Allison:
It is not really having the same skill set. You need to fill each step of the team with a compatible skill set. Everybody has to have a piece of the puzzle that makes a complete team.

Shannon:
How have mentors in your real estate investing helped you to navigate potential pitfalls?

Scott:
Oh, having someone there to help guide you is huge. A mentor is always there to answer questions for you and give you the extra boost of confidence that some days you really need when you have the little voice in your head, you know? The one that always holds you back from being your greatest self, but a little encouraging word or push from a mentor can get you closer to your dreams.

Shannon:
Allison, how does real estate allow you to earn massive and passive income?

Allison:
The massive income comes from doing fix and flips. Scott's construction background and the education we enrolled in really allowed us to utilize this strategy. It allows a quick turn on a property that we make pretty and sell quickly. Then, the passive income is the mailbox money, the rental units, having people pay you every month to live in something that you own. Scott and I have tenants who go to work every day to pay us rent. That has allowed us to acquire 35 units in 7 years. It's a great sense of security for us to open the mailbox every month and have those rent checks to deposit.

Shannon:
When doing a fix and flip, what is the number one thing that you want to look out for?

Scott:
Always trust your own numbers and don't believe the numbers from somebody else. Do your own due diligence. Many investors have gone down the wrong path by trusting someone else's numbers. Then, when they go to try to sell it they figure out the property isn't worth what somebody else told them it was, and they end up in a bad situation.

Shannon:
What is the best strategy for finding a fix and flip?

Allison:
I always keep my eyes open. You never know where someone is facing a real estate challenge that we just might be able to solve for them and pick up a deal in the process.

Scott:
Yeah, having a great network and just putting it out there to the world that you're always looking for deals and looking to solve others' real estate challenges. You never know who might say, 'Hey, so and so just passed away and we're trying to sell their house, or hey, I'm

behind on my mortgage. I don't know what to do. I need help, can you help me.' I mean, there's tons and tons of ways to find properties and just put it out there that you are in the business to solve others' real estate problems and challenges. People find out very quickly that you're their go-to guy or girl.

Shannon:
If someone wanted to invest in multi-family dwellings, what do they need to know?

Scott:
Average rents in your area would be a great start. That tells you how much you are able to pay for a building. It'll tell you how much money you have coming in every month. Then, the number of units that you will have. Units will determine your rent base. Then you really need to know your area and the type of tenants you will have. That will determine how much time you will need to manage a property or whether or not you will choose to hire a manager or do the managing yourself.

Shannon:
Allison, what is cash flow, and why should it be such an important focus of your business?

Allison:
Cash flow is what's left at the end of the day. Cash flow is what puts gas in the car, food on the table, and the bills paid to keep your business running.

Shannon:
Why do you think that people fail at real estate investing?

Scott:
They don't do their own homework and due diligence. They rely on somebody else to tell them what a property is worth, and they try to take shortcuts and not believe in their gut feeling. They try to let people influence their decisions and not be as proactive in running the numbers. It's well known that there are people out there who all they're trying to do is make a quick buck off of somebody, and if

you're not doing your homework and due diligence you could fall victim to that.

Allison:
One of the other problems is because people think they know it all. They don't listen to other people's suggestions. They aren't open to learning new ideas and new ways of doing things, so if you go in thinking you know it all and consider yourself invincible, you're probably going to fail.

Shannon:
Is real estate investing dependent on a strong economy?

Scott:
Oh, absolutely not. We bought some of our best properties when the economy was in the tank. The general consensus is to position yourself to be able to buy when the economy is in bad shape. You know, the big crash helped educate investors to prepare themselves to be in a good position so that when the economy does take a dive you're in a position to acquire more and better properties to set yourself up for the long haul.

Shannon:
What is one example of an investment strategy that is good to use in a weak economy?

Scott:
I would say in a weak economy when people are struggling and are barely making ends meet, a subject to is a great one. People just get in over their heads, and they don't know what to do in their situation. You can show them how you can help catch them up on their payments and get them caught up with the bank and save them from a short sale or a foreclosure. That's been a great strategy with many of the investors in our community. It's possible to do wonderful things with the subject to strategy.

Shannon:
What is a good strategy for acquiring properties in a strong economy?

Scott:

In a strong economy, sales are a little more complex unless you have the cash to go out and overpay for properties like most uneducated investors do. But seller financing is a great strategy for when the economy is strong. People have properties for decades and they think they're worth a lot, which sometimes is true, but what they don't realize is to sell this property outright the IRS is going to be having their hands out waiting for capital gains taxes on what they just earned. So, we show them by seller financing they can keep more of their equity and savings from their sale. Selling the property over time is huge for people to avoid that big hit from capital gains.

Shannon:

How has your education in real estate investing changed the way that you invest?

Scott:

Well, I had never invested before. I was always just a hammer swinger, and so learning to invest for me was about the purchase process. I knew the process of how to fix things, but I never knew how to purchase these properties that we were going to sell, or I was going to rent to others. With the purchasing puzzle piece in place, the education taught me how to analyze and acquire properties correctly in an entity so that its shielded from my personal assets. That's been huge for us, having your personal assets protected from the business assets is just Business 101 but most property owners don't follow this and allow themselves to be subject to somebody on the sidewalk slipping and falling or something crazy like that.

We have everything structured in a place that protects everything we have personally. Well, as well as they can be from any frivolous lawsuits.

Shannon:

Most millionaires and billionaires have investment in commercial real estate. Why do you think that is?

Scott:

Well, commercial properties command higher dollar rents so the returns are greater, and in the big picture, that's where the big money's at, so it's nice to have a few commercial properties. But they require the relationships where you can obtain the bigger dollars to purchase, and if done properly they return the bigger dollars in your mailbox money.

Shannon:
How can a real estate investor benefit from a lease option?

Scott:
The lease option is the ability to rent a house out and purchase it over time. In a short or a declining market, the lease option gives the owner the ability to postpone the sale or project a sales price years down the road when the market improves, and the property will fetch a higher sales price, but yet it allows the perspective owner to rent the property until the time that they exercise their option to purchase the property. If the property does not appraise for the option value, the buyers are not required to exercise the option to purchase the property. You're trying to forecast the market improving, but if the appraisal doesn't go up to the option price the renter doesn't have to exercise their option at the higher price. The property isn't valued at that higher price. It no longer appraises at that, so the buyer doesn't have to pay the option price.

Shannon:
Is there really a risk to the investor or the seller on a lease option, or is that really a no-lose situation for them?

Scott:
As the buyer of an option, they're pretty much in a good position. If their property depreciates to less than the option price they don't have to purchase the property. On the flip side, the seller, when the time comes to exercise the option and the property appraises for more than their projected option price, does not have the ability of raising the sale price. They have to stick with what they projected the option would be at the time of sale thus the ability to properly forecast the market values in a lease option is a very important skill to allow you to be profitable in using this strategy. It's a win-win for everybody.

Shannon:
When doing a short sale, what is something that you should anticipate?

Scott:
It takes a long time. A lot of headaches with the bank.

Shannon:
How long do they usually take from beginning to end?

Scott:
They could take anywhere from as short as 90 days to over a year and a half. It all depends on the bank. The asset managers at the banks really control how long it takes to process the information.

Shannon:
Allison, how has real estate investing changed your life?

Allison:
It's changed our life by adding a sense of security. We go to bed knowing that no matter what it's going to be okay. Scott has a whole new outlook on life being a business owner and running a company and it's just grown us in ways we never anticipated. I can't wait until the next couple of years. It's going to give us even more freedom than what we've already have experienced to this point.

Shannon:
Scott, how about you?

Scott:
Yeah, again, I'd say the ability to sleep at night. You know there are 35 families going to work every day to put money in your mailbox, and if you lose a vacancy here or there it's not going to affect you in a drastic way unlike having a W-2 and being laid off. It gives you a heightened security and just the time and freedom to be able to do what you want, when you want, with who you want. That's the Holy Grail. You know, that thing that ultimately, we would like to achieve.

Allison:
I feel like it's also given us a large sense of gratitude as well, because we provide housing to homeless veterans and work with many of the area's social services. Gratitude, but its filled with humility—to give somebody a nice home to live in, you know? Some of our tenants lived on the streets for years and have never lived in a place as nice

as we provide. It's just really enlightening and extremely humbling to see how the other parts of the world have lived. We had no idea, but now that we're able to give them a decent place to live it is pretty amazing.

Shannon:
What type of legacy do you want to leave?

Scott:
Well, I have thought about that a lot, and to be very honest, to know that I can set up to provide for our daughter and our daughter's children and have it last generations after that. To be able to provide for them 70-100 years down the road and to know that that's the type of thing that we are actually working on is very humbling, very satisfying. It's just really neat when you think of more than just yourself and just what's here now, what's going to happen in the future, and not 10-20 years in the future and not just my daughter's future, but for generations to come.

Allison:
I want to add that we're giving our daughter a future that we weren't exposed to. We were taught to go to school, get good grades, go to college, get a job, and work for 40 years and after that, if you survived, retire on 40 percent of what you made while you were working. She already knows that's not the way life has to happen. That's the best thing we can pass along to her. She comes with us to workshops and property tours; she helps us work on properties. She is learning how to be her own boss and own her own time. She already knows that what they teach you in school is not all the tools that you need to know to be successful. We weren't given the opportunities that she has already learned at the age of 14.

Candie Baker De Jong

Candie Baker De Jong grew up on the south side of Chicago with her parents and younger brother. From a young age, her parents taught her the value of hard work and the importance of family. For the first decade of her life, Candie's mother raised her while her father worked as an interior designer; he also taught color theory, and this helped Candie to develop her artistic sense. Her mother later went on to work as many as three jobs at once to help support the family. Candie credits her mother for her ability to persevere through life's many challenges, for teaching her that everything is achievable when you believe in yourself.

Candie went on to complete two years at Columbia College in downtown Chicago studying graphic arts. At the age of twenty, she left school to settle down and start a family, marrying in 1984 and soon after pursuing her real estate license. She got her start at one of the largest property management companies in Chicago and eventually was promoted to leasing director where her passion for real estate flourished. But knowing that she wanted more time to be a mom, she set aside her pursuit of real estate to raise her two boys Matthew and Jacob. During this time, she also started and ran a retail business with her husband.

In early 2000, after her divorce, Candie found herself a single mother facing the challenge of raising her two boys while trying to jump back into the work force. She began searching for a flexible opportunity that allowed her to be with her kids while also earning a comfortable living. Reverting back to her past experiences, she realized that the flexible job she was looking for was in real estate investing. In 2004, Candie sought her first opportunities in that field and began to look for investments with her current husband, Ken De Jong, later that year. With Candie's knowledge of real estate and Ken's experienced construction background, together they completed their first fix and flip in 2007. With the decline of the market and economy in 2008, they learned their early lessons the hard way. When Candie realized she still lacked certain knowledge, she searched for an investment in education that would mitigate her risks. Her search led her to one of the top-rated real estate investing educational programs in the country.

These courses covered every aspect of real estate investing as well as financial literacy and other avenues of wealth creation. Learning from her earlier experiences, she was able to understand the value of collaboration with other expert investors and entrepreneurs. Since then, Candie has successfully flipped and rehabbed eight houses, built numerous rental portfolios, and partnered with over a dozen investors raising over a million dollars in funding. She is now an award-winning real estate investor and has received recognition on both the regional and national level.

Today, Candie has realized her dream of being able to raise her boys while excelling in the real estate investing field. She hopes to pass on her knowledge to her kids and the next generation as she continues to grow as an investor.

Shannon:

According to Forbes magazine, real estate is one of the top three ways people become wealthy. As a real estate expert, why do you feel this is the case?

Candie:

I feel real estate investing is one of the top three ways that people become wealthy for a number of reasons. For one, it is a never-ending world of opportunity. Real estate is in our lives one way or another, you just may not be aware of it. People will always need a place to live, eat, and sleep whether they are renting or own their home. They are on one end of the real estate transaction or the other. Buildings, houses, places for people to work, eat, shop, relax, vacation, and learn; every aspect of our lives is touched by a piece of land or property. It is constantly changing, growing, and evolving as we do, therefore it's necessary. Let's face it, someone has to know how to develop, build, and control those properties.

The other reason is that ANYONE who has the guts to keep an open mind, isn't too proud to admit that they DO NOT know everything and are willing to invest the time necessary to educate themselves and become an expert in real estate investing strategies can do it.

Shannon:

What inspired you to get into real estate?

Candie:

I think it was a combination of inspiration and realization.

The inspiration to become whatever I chose to be, in my case a real estate investor, came from my parents, especially my mom. We didn't have much money growing up, but whenever my brother or I wanted something, we weren't told we "can't afford it." Instead my Mom would say, "Let's figure out how we can do that." So that's what I did.

The realization came in to play with my childhood. I grew up in the inner city of Chicago in a little apartment; we moved a number of times, and the one constant thing was that whatever house we lived in was not ours—we didn't own it. My parents were paying rent to someone else. Somebody got the money for that house, and it wasn't us. It went from our pockets into theirs.

I think I realized that when I started playing *Monopoly* as a kid. In *Monopoly*, you learn how you can make money and build wealth passively through buying houses and hotels and controlling properties. That's when I decided that when I grew up I would be the one to collect the rent and not pay it to someone else like my parents had done. I watched my Mom and Dad save money to buy a house only to have to use it to survive when my Dad was laid off from his job. Sound familiar? I didn't want that for my future family.

Shannon:

If someone wanted to get started in real estate, what would you recommend they do first?

Candie:

From my experience, I would recommend connecting with a large community or group of real estate investors. I did it the hard way when I first started out. Don't choose just any community or any real estate investing group but one that is well educated, knowledgeable, and currently investing in real estate. A group that is consistent, one that works together and has a good support and educational system.

I would then suggest that they plan on educating themselves in every aspect of real estate investing. Start with researching different strategies, and choose one based on that person's strong suit as well as what fits their current situation. Choose one to start, learn every aspect of that particular strategy, gain as much knowledge as possible about it, and become an expert. I would then recommend that they continue to add additional strategies in the same way, paying close attention to their current market conditions as well as their overall plan. Build and grow each strategy to enhance their portfolio, becoming an expert at one before they move on to the next. You don't want to get stuck in one strategy or grow too quickly. Getting pigeonholed is the wrong way to go.

Shannon:

How has your education in real estate changed the way that you invest?

Candie:

Finding a comprehensive real estate investing education has been the key to longevity and being a successful real estate investor. Being educated has stopped me from making many of the mistakes that novice investors make. I speak from experience. I did a flip prior to really educating myself. I had a background in real estate as well as business ownership; I was a realtor in the 1980s when interest rates were 18 percent to 24 percent. I worked for a property management company as leasing director, then left that to start a small retail business. I thought with my background and experience, and by adding more knowledge through reading, taking a boot camp, coaching, etc., that it would be enough to start doing real estate deals. Let's face it, I wanted the gold before I knew how to mine for it. What I discovered was two things: 1) My previous knowledge and experience weren't even the tip of the iceberg. 2) I didn't know what I didn't know. I couldn't intelligently ask the proper questions or research a subject if I wasn't aware it was out there in the first place.

I did my first deal in 2007, before the crash. I did some things right, but I did so much wrong. I learned through the hard knocks in life because I wasn't educated . . . and it cost me more than any education could have.

Since then, I've found a good solid real estate investing education and a fantastic investing group. I've invested in the six inches between my ears. Education has opened my eyes to so many different aspects of investing, financial literacy, and wealth building. Now I keep up on the trends and market conditions; I continue to grow and learn different strategies. I've discovered the importance of a good foundation, in business as well as real estate investing. I have been able to take real estate investing to the next level, and really there's no direction that I can't go in. I have exposure to commercial, land development, multi-family, seller-finance noted, subject to, tax liens, and short sales to name a few. Then there are other strategies like retirement account investing for your business, as well as for you personally, that I didn't even know existed.

Shannon:
What do you think is the number one mistake an individual makes when buying their first investment property?

Candie:
The number one mistake I feel people make when buying their first investment property is thinking that they know more than they really do. When I first started, that's what I thought too. I learned a valuable expensive lesson on that first flip, and I learned it the hard way.

I have heard so many people say that going to a library and studying up on it or going to a two-day boot camp is enough to be able to analyze and flip a property properly. People watch the HGTV shows and think that they can do a flip as easily as they make it seem like on TV, not realizing there's so much more to it. Real estate investing is an extremely risky business and the best way to mitigate that risk is through knowledge and education. Get out of your own way and be open to understanding and learning about what you don't know.

Shannon:

How do you minimize the risk of investing so that you can maximize your success?

Candie:

The main way I minimize risk and maximize success is to surround myself with professionals who are experts in their field. Building a solid group of professionals on my team is crucial. Support through other investors is so important. I've done real estate on my own before, and I now know the value in finding an ethical, well-educated group of investors that collaborate and support each other instead of competing. Constantly learning and growing through continuous education, keeping up on the ever-changing market, and surrounding myself with like-minded entrepreneurs and real estate investors has been key. You must be creative, willing to grow, to learn, and be open to different ideas. Create a solid foundation for your real estate investing business. Be sure you have the proper entity structure in place for the type of investing you are doing. Education is a lifetime formula for minimizing risk and maximizing success.

Shannon:

How have mentors in your real estate investing helped you to navigate potential pitfalls?

Candie:

Having instructors and mentors that are currently investing in the strategy or strategies you are interested in pursuing is crucial in helping you navigate potential pitfalls. I've found that every deal is different. No two deals are alike, and you will come across many challenges as you invest. Having an expert mentor to collaborate with has saved me time, money, and gray hairs. I've learned so much from other's experiences with their deals. Real estate investing really is a team sport.

The first deal I did was pretty much on my own. I didn't have anyone to go to for advice. I made so many mistakes from the beginning of that deal to the very end, even though I had some experience in real estate and my partner was a general contractor. Back then, we never could have imagined some of the things that went wrong or that we did wrong. Hindsight is 20/20 and looking back, I now realize that so many of those mistakes could have been avoided had we had some support and proper training. To be able to tap into an experienced seasoned investor who is currently successful in today's market makes a world of difference. After that first deal, I searched for the right training and a knowledgeable group of investors to learn from and to plug into. Since I found the right combination, we no longer are alone to make mistakes but instead collaborate on a regular basis with experts as we grow our investing business.

Shannon:
What are some creative ways to acquire a property?

Candie:
I have a few favorites. The first would be 'subject to' purchases. Purchasing 'subject to' means buying the property subject to the existing mortgage. This works well when a seller just wants out of their house. Usually the homeowner is in some sort of distress. It could be a job loss or transfer, or it may be that someone passed away and they don't or can't emotionally deal with the property. They usually don't want to wait for the house to sell in any traditional ways (for sale by owner or on the MLS). It's a burden to them, so you basically take over their existing mortgage payments. You also see more 'subject to' deals happening when current interest rates are high and the homeowner's interest rate is lower. That could mean a huge savings monthly.

Another creative way is retirement account investing: using your retirement account to acquire properties and invest in real estate. You can only do this when you have a true self-directed retirement account. This is done using a third-party administrator and there are only a handful of companies that do this. Instead of investing in stocks, bonds, or mutual funds, you direct the administrator to purchase the investment property of your choice. You can have a rental property in your retirement account fueling it with the rental income or you can do a flip or wholesale in the retirement account. You would analyze the deals to be sure they are good investments. You can also partner with other investors for larger properties. This way I am investing my retirement account in something I know and understand instead of the stock market that I am less familiar with and is less stable.

The third way is seller financing or seller carrybacks. You would pay the seller a down payment and they would then carry back all or part of the note or seller finance the purchase. They act as the bank. What I like about this is the investor doesn't have to come out of pocket for the full purchase price or secure conventional funding by dealing with traditional lenders. This works great with a multi-family property that needs a ton of work. You can secure seller financing for the duration of the rehab and once it is tenanted and has a rental history, the investor can refinance the property, pay off the previous owner financing, and take out cash to do more projects.

You can get really creative and combine these. I love puzzles, especially when you can be creative by combining strategies and solve challenges in order to make it a win-win situation for all parties.

Shannon:
So, you said that there are people who have the properties, and you acquire them. Where do you find those people and properties?

Candie:
Some of the best ways I've found properties has been through word of mouth or through networking with other groups and Investors. My husband and I currently have a property that we are in negotiations on that came through a friend of a friend. Another way is to look at online sites like craigslist, for sale by owner sites, or better yet the county websites for foreclosures, divorces, and deaths. It may sound morbid, but those are the people that need my help most. They are not only in emotional destress but financial distress as well and are looking for a way out. When my mom passed away, if I wasn't an investor, I know I would have been relieved to talk to someone that had another option for me other than listing my mom's properties with a realtor. Newspapers are also an excellent resource to find people wanting to sell properties for sale by owner. Not to mention the legal section. These are all fantastic ways to find people who have distressed properties for sale

before they are listed on the MLS. Once the property hits the MLS, they're going to be picked through quickly. Now, I've found my fair share of great deals on the MLS. That's where having a good realtor on your team has worked extremely well in finding those gems. The idea is to find and acquire the property before it hits the market. Resources and a strong network are key.

Shannon:
Do you feel that real estate investing success is dependent on a stronger economy?

Candie:
No not necessarily. Real estate investing can be done in any economy as long as you are keeping up with the changes in the market and adjusting your strategy accordingly. Look at 2005-06 when the economy was strong. Property values were through the roof. Everyone wanted to invest in real estate. Back then as long as you could fog a mirror you could get financing. But the question is, was it the time to buy or the time to sell? When the economy and the real estate market are like that, it's the time to sell not necessarily buy. As an investor, the general rule of thumb is to sell high and buy low. A year or so later, when the economy tanked, and property values plummeted, people were being laid off from their jobs and were losing their homes to foreclosure. Many investors lost their shirts as well, mainly because they over leveraged themselves. Before the bottom of the market dropped out, many refinanced their properties and cashed out their equity to do more deals. They were unaware or unprepared for the shift that was coming in 2008. Markets change at their own pace and sometimes sneak up on you if you're not paying attention. As an investor, the key to success in any economy is having many strategies in your pocket so you can shift into the strategy that makes the most sense for that economy.

Shannon:
In your business, how do you help others learn more about real estate?

Candie:
I love to help people, especially those that have a thirst for knowledge and want to learn to invest properly. It's so very important that they make the right choice when deciding on an investing education. Our

investing group has monthly real estate workshops where we bring in instructors to train on the strategy that they are experts in. When I come across someone wanting to learn and see what the classes are like, I invite them down to join us. I've also held property tours at my projects and given people a chance to see what a live flip or rehab is like. I go over the deal: How I found the property. How the deal was structured and funded. What we are planning on doing to increase the value. Lastly what the projected profit is. I'll answer any question they have. If it is a tour that is done after the project is completed, I talk about the pitfalls and challenges I came across and how I handled them. Another way I help others learn about real estate investing is through a webinar. I am currently doing a short webinar for people to get information about the education and training that I took to become a real estate investor. They are always welcome to join me at other events, and I'm happy to sit down with them and help them any way I can.

Shannon:
What is cash flow, and why is it so important to your business?

Candie:
Cash flow is basically the money that flows in and out of your business. Money comes in as income and goes out as expenses. What is left over after you pay your expenses is either positive or negative. Positive cash flow is when you have more coming in than going out. Negative cash flow is when you have more debt going out than income coming in. Cash flow is important for any business. It is your business's lifeblood. Positive cash flow is obviously better than negative. It shows your business is running well. The more cash flow you have, the more capable and flexible your business is to make larger investments, obtain conventional financing, and propel your business forward. Not to mention it keeps the shareholders happy when you have a larger company. Now I'm not an accountant or tax advisor, but depending on your business model and what your end goal is, some investors feel showing negative cash flow on your taxes can be as beneficial as positive cash flow in your day-to-day business. This may sound confusing—how can negative cash flow be a benefit? As a real estate investor and small business owner, we have far more write offs and deductions that we can take on our taxes than a W-2 employee can. Based on what is most important to your business, an investor

may choose to take as many deductions as possible in order to pay as little as possible in taxes legally. That doesn't mean the business doesn't make money, it just looks like it's losing money on paper because of all the write offs. By saving more on your taxes, you have less money physically going out in taxes, keeping more in your pocket. This works well for real estate investing when you have private lenders or partners that you work with on a regular basis and do not have to obtain more traditional financing for your deals. Again, the downside is that showing negative cash flow can hinder your business from obtaining conventional financing for larger deals.

Shannon:

How does real estate allow you to earn massive and passive income?

Candie:

Real estate investing is the one avenue where one can earn massive as well as passive income while taking advantage of the many deductions and tax write offs that are available to property owners and businesses.

What's wonderful about real estate is that there are so many strategies you can implement to create wealth, not to mention you don't need a lot of starting capital in order to make money in real estate investing. What you do need is the knowledge and know-how to implement deals and build your income effectively and efficiently.

You can massively and passively acquire wealth through your holdings whether it be through flipping or single-family to multi-family rentals, as well as commercial and land development. You can implement financial strategies to pay down any mortgage you may have on your properties quicker using your same income. This allows you to save money on interest and keep more money in your pocket. You also earn massive and passive income through appreciation in real estate, through depreciation/write offs, and rental income. The goal is to diversify your portfolio and continually build on your investing strategy so that when something comes across your desk, you can act on it and not miss out on an opportunity. Real estate investing is so versatile it's really up to you the direction you want to go. As long as you're armed with the knowledge and work with the right group of people, you can take anything on.

Shannon:
*If someone wanted to invest into multi-family dwellings, what do they
need to know that's different than a single-family home?*

Candie:
Investing in multi-family is different than single-family rentals.
There are pros and cons to both strategies. First off, you have to analyze multi-family properties differently. You look at the cap rate with
multi-family vs using a CMA (comparative market analysis) as you do
with single-family rentals. The amount of capital you will need to
raise for a multi-family will be much higher than the money needed
to acquire and rehab single family rentals. Remember, you're doing
multiple rehabs in one building. Be aware that in multi-family there
are other ways of increasing your income besides rent. Things like
coin-operated laundry facilities, charging for garage space, etc. With
multi-family rentals, you have all your rentals in one place unlike
single family rentals that are usually scattered. You also save time
and money when you have your rentals in one building. You may
have 6, 10, 20 plus units in one building, on one piece of land, with
only one roof, one basement, one tax bill, one yard, and other ongoing
expenses that need to be taken care instead of multiple expenses with
more than one property. Thus, maximizing the performing asset
while minimizing their on-going costs. There's more competition with
multi-family rentals; there are more out there to choose from vs single-family rentals that are usually rented by people who are looking
for a longer-term rental, and there are typically less to choose from
depending on the area. When you have a vacancy in a multi-family, it
doesn't affect you as much as having a single-family vacancy. You
still have income from other units that are rented to pay your expenses. Multi-families can require more property management due to it
being more transient than someone renting a three-bedroom home.
These are a few of the differences between the two.

Shannon:
*What is one of the things that you look for in a property when you're do-
ing a rehab?*

Candie:
The one thing that I look for when considering a property to rehab is
hidden space. This would include outdoor living space which is huge

now. I'm looking to create additional living space without changing the original footprint. This keeps the rehab cost down and the taxes from going up for the future homeowner. It also gives me the best bang for my buck. I look for hidden potential: ways to open up the floor pan, a porch that can be converted into a larger kitchen or family room, a den or unfinished basement that can be turned into an open concept kitchen and family room or lower level rec room, extra bedroom and bath, or office. I've taken a five-room home with two bedrooms, one and a half baths, and no family room and turned it into a seven-room home with three bedrooms, three and a half baths, a main level family room, and a lower level rec room. I achieved this by rearranging the living space upstairs to create three good size bathrooms and added a master bath. I converted an enclosed back porch to a family room and opened it up to the kitchen and dining room to get the open concept that everyone loves. I finished the basement and added a full bath with a with a lower level rec room. I purchased this property for $152,000, rehab and holding costs were close to $183,000, and I sold it for $425,000 cash within a six-month period.

Shannon:
Most millionaires and billionaires have investments in commercial real estate. Why?

Candie:
Commercial real estate takes an investor to another level. Millionaires and billionaires invest in commercial real estate for a number of reasons. In most cases these are businesses that are well established that are leasing from you. This is their livelihood. They're in it for the long term. They are not as transient as other types of tenants. Commercial leases differ from residential leases in that they offer flexibility for both the landlord and the tenant. There are three basic types of lease, some may be more landlord friendly than others. Some tax advantages are depreciation of the asset. Depreciation can offset the cash flow from rental income. Depreciation can be accelerated by cost segregation, which can increase immediate cash flow. A simple example of the overall principle of cost segregation is that a dollar is worth less tomorrow than what a dollar is worth today. When you sell the property and there is a true capital gain, the gains are taxed at the long-term capital gain rate which is usually lower than the ordinary income rate.

Shannon:
How can a real estate investor benefit from a tax deed?

Candie:
Benefits of a tax lien or tax deed will be different depending on the state an investor decides to invest in. Some states are tax lien states while others are tax deed states. Investors can either collect interest on the tax lien that they purchase or acquire that property if the owner does not bring the taxes current or both. As an investor in a tax lien state, the investor bids on a tax lien certificates usually at a tax lien auction that goes to the highest bidder. The investor will collect interest on the lien from the homeowner until the homeowner brings the taxes current. Homeowner redemption periods and Interests rates vary from state to state. If the homeowner cannot bring their taxes current plus interest within a certain amount of time, the investor then forecloses on that property and now owns it. Whereas in a tax deed state, when a homeowner doesn't pay their taxes, the government has the right to take that property and sell it at a tax deed sale. The purchaser of that tax deed then receives that property and now owns it. Each state will be different so be sure you understand how your state works. Either way, tax liens and tax deeds are a great way to invest. In many cases the out of pocket for the investor is small compared to other types of investing.

Shannon:
What type of legacy do you want to leave?

Candie:
The legacy that I would love to leave isn't necessarily monetary. I've never been one to spoil my boys. I believed that everyone should work for what they want and then feel the pride of accomplishing it. What I want to give back is teaching our younger generation about the value in keeping an open mind; the value in working hard for something that they really want, enjoy, and see a future in; and understanding the value of financial literacy, business ownership, and entrepreneurialism. This country was built by small businesses. We got away from that for a while. Now I see a huge resurgence in small businesses, especially work-from-home businesses. I want our youth to have the career they want and also know that there are other options out there that could give them pride in building something of

their own, give them more time and financial freedom than building something for someone else. I want them to understand the value of owning and running a small business and all the benefits that come with it. Lastly, I want to leave them with the legacy of financial literacy, knowing how to invest their money wisely and make good decisions for themselves and their families.

Jill Nettesheim

As a child, Jill Nettesheim had lemonade stands and candy stores, and she was always jotting down business ideas and drawings in a notebook. She loved the idea of having her own business one day. Growing up, her father and her mother instilled in her that it was really important to go to school, to get good grades, and to get into college, so that she could get a good job. So that's what Jill did. She held positions within the banking and financial industry for most of her life but still found herself wanting her own business. Throughout her career, Jill had dabbled as an entrepreneur in several multi-level marketing companies but never felt passionate about them. As she bought and sold a few homes throughout the years, Jill found herself watching rehab shows and collecting pictures of what she wanted in a home. It wasn't until she actually renovated a few of her own that she realized how exciting it was and how much satisfaction it gave her. Jill decided to learn more about real estate and since then has started her own real estate business and is currently partnering in deals with other real estate investors.

Shannon:

According to Forbes magazine, real estate is one of the top three ways people become wealthy. As a real estate expert, why do you feel this is the case?

Jill:

By investing in real estate, there are lots of ways to generate wealth on a piece of property. For example, there's cash flow, appreciation, equity, and tax benefits. These four wealth generators combined are very powerful.

Shannon:

What is cash flow and why should it be such an important focus of your business?

Jill:

Cash flow is the extra profit left over after all expenses have been paid on a property. For example, if you have a duplex bringing in $2,200 in rental income, and your expenses are $1,800, the remaining amount is your cash flow. So even though it doesn't seem like $400 is a lot of money, if you had maybe 5, 10, or 20 properties like that, it adds up. You need cash flow in order to pay business expenses and expand your business.

Shannon:

Can you elaborate on why appreciation, equity, and tax benefits help build real estate wealth as well?

Jill:

You can gain appreciation in several ways. Your property may not appreciate in value every year, but over the long run, properties generally increase in value, and that means you can sell the property for more than you what purchased it for. If you make repairs to the property, you've added appreciation value to the property. Also, if you have a rental property, over the long run, rent tends to appreciate, so you may be able to charge higher rents, depending on what area you're in.

Equity is also a wealth builder. If you take out a loan when you purchase the property, when you make your loan payment each month, you're paying down both principle and interest and thereby increasing your equity in that property. Equity is the difference between what a property is worth and what is owed on it. So as long as your property value doesn't drop, your equity increases.

And then there are the tax benefits. By owning property versus owning a regular business, you're not charged self-employment taxes. By owning real estate, you can also receive depreciation deductions, and when you sell your properties, they're taxed at long-term capital gains rates, which are lower than short-term rates.

Shannon:
What inspired you to get into real estate?

Jill:
I've always wanted to have a business of my own. I just never knew what it was I wanted to do. Nothing really got me excited. Throughout the years I purchased a few homes and began thinking about what it would be like to rehab properties. I found myself saving photos and inspiring articles, but it wasn't until I remodeled a couple of my properties that I actually thought about doing it as a career. It was so exciting seeing something ugly turn into something beautiful. That's when I started looking into real estate seriously.

Shannon:
If someone were to come to you and they wanted to start investing in real estate, what would you recommend they do first?

Jill:
Without a doubt, you should educate yourself first, and that not only means education in real estate, but it also means educating yourself in financial literacy. You need to know how to correctly set up your corporations and LLCs, and improve your business credit and your personal credit. You also need to figure out what your investor ID is. That means that you need to figure out what you are good at, who you want to sell to, and what your goals are before you start going out and doing real estate. Otherwise, you're just wasting your time, and you could potentially make costly mistakes.

Someone interested in real estate should also start attending real estate networking events and then start building relationships with people they meet. By doing that, you can find out who you want to work with. You want to find people that are good at what you aren't good at.

Another important thing to think about when you start is what is your "why"? Knowing what your "why" is will help you stay committed to your dreams and goals. Many people get into real estate just thinking about how much money they'll make, but money rarely is enough reason to keep you committed.

Shannon:
What is one of the top real estate strategies that you have learned?

Jill:
I don't have a top or favorite anything. If you ask me my favorite color, it may be purple one day and green the next. Or my favorite music. I listen to many types of music. I don't have a top real estate strategy at this point, but I do know that whatever I do, it needs to fit into my investor ID. Right now, my focus is investing in fix and flip or rehab deals through my self-directed IRA, but tomorrow it might be different.

Shannon:
What's your favorite ice cream flavor?

Jill:
LOL. I don't eat much ice cream, and again, I don't have a favorite, but I do remember as a child I loved mint chocolate chip! Yum.

Shannon:
When you began your real estate investing career, how important was it for you to establish a team to help you be successful?

Jill:
A team is very important. You need to establish a team of people with whom you'll work well with. You want people on your team whom you trust and people that think like you do. And you'll want to establish these relationships before you begin a deal so that, when the deal comes, you have this team at your fingertips. For example, if you need a plumber or an electrician or are trying to find a buyer or a seller for a property, you have a list of individuals you can readily choose from. Others you would consider for your team could be real

estate agents, contractors, heating and cooling experts, even inground pool experts!

Shannon:

How have mentors in your real estate investing helped you to navigate potential pitfalls?

Jill:

To me, my mentors have been very, very helpful. They're there to encourage you, to support you, and they're people whom you can learn from and bounce ideas off of. They're also able to help you look at things from an outside viewpoint.

We're taught that you shouldn't do real estate emotionally, to leave emotion out of it. You have to know your goals and when to say yes and when to say no. Here's an example of how a mentor has helped me avoid a potentially bad decision. A few years ago, I sold a condo I had lived in for many, many years. My son grew up there from kindergarten through graduation. After he graduated, I moved on and sold the condo. A few years after that I learned the condo was in foreclosure. I got excited and talked to one of my mentors about buying it back.

He said, "Well, why? Why would you want to do that?" After thinking about it, I thought, "Well, yeah, why do I want to do that?" I realized I was basing my decision emotionally and not considering my goals and desired outcomes.

Another advantage to having mentors is that they can help steer you clear of mistakes that they may have made. It's much easier to learn from others' mistakes than making your own.

Shannon:

Why is it a mistake to buy a property when you are emotional about it?

Jill:

It may cause you to make mistakes. You want to do a deal that is going to help you reach your goals and a deal that makes sense from a numerical standpoint. If it doesn't help you reach your goals or the numbers don't make sense, then don't do the deal.

Shannon:

When doing a fix and flip, what is one of the number one things that you want to look out for?

Jill:

I think an important aspect of fix and flips is to make sure that you've done your due diligence. You want to make sure that the deal is structured correctly so that all parties are protected and that your numbers make sense. Make sure the comps you pull are in the same neighborhood as the property and that the homes are similar in features to your property after you've done your rehab. Comps can vary a lot depending on what street the property is on or what neighborhood the property is in. You also need to ensure that you have evaluated the market. You need to know what the market is doing. Is it a hot market? Is it a cold market? What's the area like? What's the neighborhood like? What is the job market like in that area? So, you need to know all of those things in order to effectively and successfully figure out if you should do that fix and flip.

Shannon:

What is one of the strategies that you've used for finding a fix and flip?

Jill:

My strategy of finding fix and flips has been through networking. I'm involved in a very large real estate group. I found my first deals through networking in the group. However, there are many other ways to find deals, such as online websites, Facebook groups, and real estate agents.

Shannon:

How can an individual benefit from a lease option?

Jill:

Lease options are a great strategy. A lease option gives the tenant the right to purchase the property at the end of the lease. Their lease payments can be applied toward the purchase price. This benefits the tenant or buyer if they are not able to qualify for a mortgage or don't have a down payment or good credit. They may be new to the neighborhood. A lease option also gives them an opportunity to live in that neighborhood for a while to determine if they really want to live there. Or they may be relocating and are waiting to sell their previous property to fund a new property purchase. If for any reason, they are just not ready to purchase, they can continue to lease until they are ready to buy.

Shannon:

How does an investor benefit from it then? It sounds like that's really something that an individual would benefit from more so than an investor? Is that an accurate statement?

Jill:

No. Lease options offer a great advantage for investors, or sellers, as well. If the seller wants to sell the property, they can accomplish this with a lease option. They may be able to sell the property at a higher sales price because of special financing terms they may offer the buyer. Until the time the property is sold, the seller will be receiving rent. They may also ask for higher rent in exchange for more flexible financing terms. If the buyer decides not to purchase, the seller is able to keep the non-refundable deposit. Another advantage is that the seller doesn't need to engage a real estate agent and can then avoid agent fees. And while the seller still owns the home, they are entitled to tax benefits. So, it's really a win-win for both the buyer and the investor.

Shannon:

When doing a short sale, what should you anticipate?

Jill:

You can anticipate that a short sale is not going to be so short. I'm not sure why they were named that way, but it usually takes a good amount of time to purchase a short sale property. It may go quickly, three months, but it usually goes much longer than that. If the investor needs to close by a particular date, a short sale would not be a good strategy for them. They should anticipate that the transaction will not close until the seller's mortgage lender agrees to the sale. There may be roadblocks which can sidetrack a short sale, so the investor should do their research ahead of time. Also, the investor will be buying the property "as is," so they should be prepared to make repairs on the property, sometimes extensively. They should also be prepared for the possibility that that the short sale may fall through.

The seller of the property usually has to pay money at closing or agree to an unsecured debt in order to have the short sale approved. If the seller refuses, then the sale may fall through even if the seller has approved the sale.

Shannon:
Why do you feel that people fail at real estate?

Jill:
I think most fail because they don't have the proper knowledge before they begin investing. If they don't have the proper knowledge, a beginning investor can make some really big mistakes which may set them back quite a bit, not only financially but emotionally as well, so that they may not continue doing real estate at all.

Shannon:
Do you feel that real estate investing success is dependent on a strong economy?

Jill:
No, I feel you can make money in a weak or a strong economy. People always need a place to live.

Shannon:
What is your favorite real estate strategy for acquiring property that you have learned?

Jill:
As I talked about previously, for fix and flips my strategy right now is networking. All my deals have been found through my real estate group. Until that well runs dry, I'll continue using that strategy.

Shannon:
How has real estate changed your life?

Jill:
I guess my life has changed in the respect that I really love what I do. I finally feel I'm doing something that actually makes a difference in people's lives. I've also developed many more relationships. It's

amazing how much easier life is when you have people that support you and think like you do.

Shannon:

What type of legacy do you want to leave?

Jill:

That's a great question. I think everyone wants to be able to create wealth and be able to leave their family enough money so that they don't have to struggle through life. I'm working toward that. In addition to that, I'd like to leave some type of legacy that benefits single and divorced mothers.

Shannon:

Why single and divorced mothers? Why does that speak to you?

Jill:

I raised my son while I was divorced. My son's father provided support, but it was still a struggle to live on a single salary. I know dads face the same problem, but I truly believe it's harder for women. I'd love to be able to help them create a legacy for their children.

Steve Nordfors

Steve Nordfors has been in the real estate industry since 1995. As a custom home builder, he has overseen projects ranging from a few thousand dollars on up to multi-million dollars. He has had the opportunity to work in multiple states across the US from a custom home on the shores of Kauai, Hawaii, to custom work for clients in San Jose, California, to multiple high end homes in the Utah market. Steve understands what it takes to get the job done and has worked well with contractors, homeowners, and city officials. He and with his wife Tammi have started multiple businesses in the real estate arena, and she is a licensed realtor with Keller Williams Legacy. Together they own businesses that work on rehabbing, rentals, consulting, construction, and marketing. Steve has been an active real estate investor since 2012. He has done single-family fix and flips, rentals, land deals, and money lending. Currently he is building his rental portfolio and continues to do fix and flips and consulting.

Shannon:
Steve, what inspired you to get into real estate?

Steve:
I have been involved in residential real estate for as long as I can re-member. My dad's a general contractor. I remember asking him at the age of eight if I could start getting paid for the work that I was doing on site. That was the just the beginning. I thoroughly enjoyed doing large custom residential homes and some small commercial work.

People would always say to me, 'Steve, you know how to do all of this stuff. Why don't you go out and build a spec house? Why don't you go out on your own and do real estate on your own?' At the time, I knew there was just so much that I didn't know. I knew how to build a house. I can build anything that anybody puts in front of me. But I knew that there were certain things that I didn't know that could wipe me out financially, such as how to fund it, what entities would hold my business to protect me and my family, and how to use the tax laws to my advantage.

Being in construction, I was able to see a broader view of the real estate industry. I love real estate and all the different ways you can make money. One day I saw a different avenue then the one I was currently on. Something that inspired me was when a friend of mine was making some additional income flipping homes. I was working on a project at the University of Utah. One of the subs told me about some of the real estate he was doing. He would show up to work eve-ry day with me, then remodel a house at night. He had just purchased this fix and flip. Over the course of time, he told me, 'We just sold it, and we made somewhere in the ballpark of $36,000 on that project.'

My love for real estate inspired me, but the fear of the unknown kept me back. My friend at the university job directed me to educa-tion to help me get past that fear. Fear that came from the lack of knowledge in the process of investing. So, I was able to transition and educate myself to be able to move forward and to be able to take my first step into the real estate investment world.

And, now, six years later, we're going strong and really having a great time with it.

Shannon:
How has your education in real estate changed the way that you invest?

Steve:

I knew that there were things out there that I didn't know. Watching other people do it, I knew that you could lose a lot of money in real estate. There are a lot of potential pitfalls, and a lot of challenges. So, to me, investing and getting educated in that arena really gave me the confidence to move forward, the ability to associate myself with other like-minded individuals, other real estate investors that have been doing it a lot longer than I have has helped too. Being able to associate with them, to run properties and projects and ideas by them, has been helpful. No one ever told me, 'No, that's not a good deal.' But they would always ask me questions that prompted me to look deeper into the numbers and inside myself to make the decision for myself.

I think that's true of anything. Whenever you endeavor to start a new career, a new life path, it's important to get the information, to get the education, the knowledge, to be able to move forward so that you understand those things that you're investing in. Because of education, we understand how to run our numbers. We know more of what to look for and what to look for in potential investments. We are now out there helping other people. I get phone calls on a regular basis asking me about different scenarios that I've been through that they're now facing. I'm able, now, to share that knowledge and information with others.

Shannon:

How have mentors in your real estate investing helped you navigate potential pitfalls?

Steve:

They've been absolutely lifesaving, financially. Because I'm able to have these mentors that have gone before, that have seen some of the challenges, that have seen some of those pitfalls, that have seen the rise and fall of the markets over time. To be able to have an individual like that is invaluable, where you can rely on them for their knowledge and then learn from them. Their experience leads to great advice, and that is also very encouraging.

Our first project that we did was with a very close mentor of ours. That really gave us the boost to go out and then do it on our own. Now, in turn, we have become a mentor and helped those who are just starting. It is great to be able to guide them and share our experience, and our knowledge, so that they can feel more confidence in their abilities to go out and invest in real estate.

Shannon:

What is the first piece of advice that you give someone who's going to get started in real estate?

Steve:

My advice is to get educated. Learn everything you can. Seek out all different avenues of learning. Read about it, study it from all angles. Whatever you are looking into doing, seek out others who have already done it and learn from them. Seek their experience and learn from it. When you have done that you can feel more confident in the decisions that you make.

For instance, my daughter wants to own and operate a tree house hotel. We have had many conversations on who she needs to have on her team and the skills she feels she would like to have. We have talked about different areas that would be important to be educated in and understand to have a successful hotel, covering education in all different aspects of the business.

So for me, when somebody's wanting to get involved in real estate, I want to tell them, 'You need to get educated in the area you want to be involved in, you need to know how to go out and do it. You can't get the information from a 30-minute TV show that comes on once a week or from a book that was written years ago. You need to get the information from reliable sources that are up to date. You need to be able to ask questions and run projects by those individuals who have been doing it for many years.'

So, get educated on the process and the potential that's there. But also, I want them to be aware of the challenges and the market. You can lose a lot of money. You can make a ton of money, which has been great. But you need to understand, get the information that you need in order to make an informed decision to move forward.

Shannon:

Is real estate investing success dependent on a strong economy?

Steve:

Absolutely not. During the time that we've been investing, we have seen a pretty steady growth in the economy. However, because of the information and the education that we continue to learn, I see different strategies and ideas where I could potentially make more money in a down economy with the ability to be able to go in and to help those individuals who are affected by the economy and are in a bind with their housing situation.

So, you can definitely make money in all markets, the rising market, the flat market, and even a declining market.

Shannon:

What are some creative ways to acquire a property in a up market?

Steve:

One of the ways that we have done some creative financing in this rising economy was when we found an individual who had owned a duplex for many years. They were struggling with tenants. On one side of the duplex a squatter was living there (meaning they were living there and not paying any rent). The other side had a family that had been there for four years without any rent increase. The owner of the duplex was out of town a lot for work, and the spouse was working a full-time job and caring for their children. They did not have time to deal with challenges that came with their investment. The duplex was becoming a burden to them. It needed some significant repairs. The foundation was sinking and needed to be lifted. It was a rough situation.

So, we were able to come to them and give them an option where we could take over the financing. We took over their payments. They kept the mortgage in their name, but we took over the obligation. We pay monthly to a third party. We were able to go in and fix up the duplex, evict the squatters, and raise the rent. We now have it rented and cash flowing monthly.

This is a strategy called a 'subject to' or seller financing. We've been doing that with several properties. This and other strategies we have learned help us to find properties and be able to finance them, even in a rising market. In a rising market, people are still struggling with the challenges of death, divorce, and loss of a job. So there are always individuals who are needing to sell property. Knowing that, there are creative ways to fund purchases can help not just the investor, but the person that needs the investor to help them out of their tough situation.

Shannon:
What are some creative ways to acquire a property in a down market?

Steve:
In a down market, often people have borrowed money on their home, and the value of that home has dropped significantly, so that they now owe more than what they could sell their house for on the open market. One of the ways that we've learned to be able to acquire homes in this particular situation is a 'short sale.' A short sale is where you approach the bank with the homeowner and ask the bank to take less, or short, of what is owed on the property.

This process is not a short process, more of a very long process, and there's a lot of paperwork and negotiations back and forth. It is a great way that you can pick up properties in a down market.

Shannon:
How long do they usually take from beginning to end?

Steve:
These can take anywhere from a couple months to over a year; it really depends on several factors: getting the paperwork in and in the right order and being able to work with the homeowner and how willing they are to work back and forth. Also, there is a lot of back and forth with the banks. It is a big process that takes lots of time and communication.

Shannon:
How has real estate changed your life?

Steve:
That is something that I will forever be grateful for. I remember working a job as a W-2 employee. The kids were growing up. I was out the door before they woke up. I was gone all day. I'd get home just in time for my wife to make dinner or reheat what she had fed the kids. We would help the kids with homework then the kids were off to bed. I didn't really have an opportunity to know my kids. I was working so much and was gone all the time, that I missed out on a lot. My wife took kids on vacations without me because I couldn't take the time off.

Now, since becoming a real estate investor and business owner, I'm able to spend time with my kids. I'm able to go on spontaneous trips. I'm there when they wake up in the morning. I can stay up late with them. They've become some of my greatest friends. I have been able to be able to interact with them, to be with them. Real estate investing has given me that opportunity.

It's also given me the opportunity to be able to work side by side with my kids. My son came to me about a year ago and said, 'Dad, how can I get my money to work for me?'

So I put it out there on social media. I was amazed at the responses. They were like, 'Well, he can come and mow my lawn.' 'He can come and clean my pool.' 'He can come and clean my windows.' And these individuals really missed the point of what my son was asking.

So my wife and I decided to show him how his money can work for him. We taught him a lesson on money lending. He is actually a money lender for me. We gave him an opportunity to put money on the duplex we bought. We agreed on terms. He didn't have a lot, but what he had is growing. He now receives a rate of return every month from the income that we make on that.

My daughter has been able to come and work with me and thoroughly enjoys that kind of hands-on work. She has been able to learn how to put in wood floors, been able to learn how to do tile back splashes, and all the other different things associated with a fix and flip and caring for our rentals.

So, for me, it has changed my life. To be able to have these experiences with my kids, to be able to teach my kids how to invest, how to work differently, how to be able to make the money work for them.

Shannon:
How does real estate allow you to earn massive and passive income?

Steve:
On the massive side, for example, my partners and I bought a piece of property that was 100 acres of land. We bought it with seller financing. We used a friend's retirement money to cover the down payment and monthly expenses. Our friend's retirement was making more money with us than traditional retirement accounts. We bought it and just sat on it for a while. We looked into the possibility of subdividing; however, with the current zoning we decided not to go with that idea. We looked into building a vacation rental or spec home on the prop-

erty. Then in the end we didn't do anything to it. We put it up for sale and sold a portion of it. Three years after we purchased, we sold the remaining portion for a combined profit of over $200,000 on that particular property.

Then, for instance, on a fix and flip. We pick up a property at a discount, then go in, make some improvements to it, and then turn around and sell it. We've made anywhere from about $3500 all the way up to $45,000 on a single transaction with a fix and flip.

And then on the passive side, you can pick up properties and hold onto them and keep them as rentals. We have rentals now that pay us on a monthly basis. That money just gets deposited directly into our bank account every single month. Or, you could do what my son is doing and lend out money and receive a rate of return on that money, backed by real estate, to be able to generate income passively that way.

Shannon:

What is cash flow? And why should it be such an important focus of your business?

Steve:

Cash flow, for me, is my lifeblood. For instance, if I have just a savings account, and I go out and I spend $30 of that savings, that $30 is gone, I spent it. But, if I have cash flow coming in, every single month, and I go out and I spend that same $30, next month that $30 is going to get replaced by that cash flow, or that stream of income.

So I believe that cash flow is the key to the lifestyle that you want. Cash flow is the key to retirement. Normal retirement accounts scare me. I don't have a retirement account at this point, unless you say that my rentals are my retirement account. I look at retirement accounts: you just put money in, put money in, put money in, and then, when you retire, you pull money out, pull money out, pull money out, pull money out. Where is that money going once you pull it out? What's replenishing that? There's nothing. It is gone. But, if you have cash flow, when you use that money, the money gets replaced. There are lots of cash flow opportunities. We like rentals and money lending, that money gets replaced every single month. Someone else works to replace that money for us. So, to me, again, cash flow is key.

Shannon:

If someone wanted to invest in multifamily dwellings, what do they need to know?

Steve:

There's a lot you need to know. Starting off, where are you going to be able to get the funds to acquire it? Those price tags are a little higher. There are options out there, seller financing, other investors, and traditional banking. You need to know how to run the numbers. You need to know what the vacancy rates are, what the NOI is, what repairs and costs you are covering as the owner, and what costs the tenants are covering.

We ran numbers on a multifamily unit and found out that the current owner did not keep good records. It was very challenging for us to be able to get those numbers. To be able to get the information and to verify the information that you're getting is vital. There's a saying, 'Trust but verify.'

We had to trust what they were giving us, but when we started to get out and verify the numbers they had given us, we realized there were some huge discrepancies. That was one of the red flags that came up to us on that one.

But again, knowing that market, knowing how to value the property, because that's totally different, valuing multi-family versus a single-family residence. You value multi-family more on the cash flow. So, when you go out to view multi-family units, understand that it's different than if you're just doing single-family. There is a lot more work involved in getting that information and going through the numbers. It is very helpful to have individuals around you to bounce ideas off of, to mentor you, to run things by, this is key when investing in multifamily.

Shannon:

When you're doing a fix and flip, what is the first thing that you want to look out for?

Steve:

The first thing I want to look out for when I'm doing a fix and flip is that I really want to know my numbers. There are things out there that could scare individuals from doing a fix and flip. You never know what you might find. We bought and had properties that we've had to go in and do some expensive cleaning and remodeling on. So it is important to look at what you are buying: Is the main structure and functions in place? Are the numbers we are running conservative or are they on the edges of possibility? We try to be very conservative so I can still make money.

And so, when we are looking at getting a fix and flip, we give ourselves some time so we can do our due diligence. We can get in the house and walk around and see if there's any issues, any structure issues, any panics. Is the roof good? How dated is the plumbing and electrical? Look at those areas where it could cost you more than you think when you get in there.

Shannon:

What is your best strategy for finding a fix and flip? Not for financing or acquiring, but how are you finding fix and flips?

Steve:
Well for us, it is our network. We really push to build our network. We let our network know what we are doing and that we have knowledge that can help with real estate struggles. We have individuals that call us and say, 'Hey, Steve, I need you to buy my house.' Or 'We have this situation, what can we do?'

We've had other individuals say, 'Hey, Steve, I need you to come help me with my house.' And then I say, 'Well, what do you need help with?' As a contractor and having experience in the residential market, a lot of people come to me for those types of things as well. But when they say, 'I need help with the house. It's just too big for me. Mom died. Brother's got cancer. We can't afford to fix it up to sell it, I need you to buy our house.' Those are opportunities for me to help my network.

And so, we're able to go in there and make them an offer. And we give them the information that they need in order to see their options. We do our best to make offers that are a win-win situation. Because of that, the best place that I have found to find fix and flip properties is by word of mouth and through our network.

Shannon:

Most millionaires and billionaires have investments in commercial real estate. Why do you think that is?

Steve:

I think it's a bigger gain. With the different options that are out there with commercial—triple net leasing, those types of things—to be able to go and buy a building and have the tenants take care of the repairs and all of those things. I think that's huge.

I think that they do it because it's a good investment. Because businesses are out there and need a place to house their business. Renting to business and those types of things, it's just playing on a bigger scale. And, I think that's why that they invest there, because that's where they can get the best return on their money.

Shannon:

How do you minimize the risk of investing so that you can maximize your success?

Steve:

Risk... that was something that scared me coming into real estate investing. I knew there were things I didn't know and that felt risky to me. When people said, 'Well, Steve, go do a spec house.' That was risky to me because I didn't have all of the information. The way that we've been able to minimize risks is getting educated. Getting information and understanding the process, and the market, to be able to take that information and make educated decisions helps to minimize the risk. Yes, there is still risk involved; however, we've been able to minimize that risk by getting educated, understanding the process, having mentors and business partners that were willing to go in it with us and take that risk as well. But they are also educated, and we have more eyes looking at it so that minimizes the risk. Also, when you educate yourself, you begin to open your mind to other possibilities. If one way doesn't work, you learn other ways that just might be the answer for that particular scenario. In real estate, the options are as creative as you are.

Shannon:

How do you think that learning multiple investing strategies protects and accelerates your investing success?

Steve:

If you only know one system, and if that system goes away, you're out of a game. To me, it's important to learn and understand multiple strategies for real estate investment, not only the buying side but the exit side, to be able to know and understand, 'If I get into a fix and flip, and something happens, what would that take for me to be able to turn that into a rental, a lease option, a seller finance?'

So, I think having multiple strategies and understanding multiple strategies really helps to minimize the risk and increase the probability that you will make money. Whatever comes up, you can resolve and you can overcome with the knowledge that you've gained by learning, not with one specific strategy but multiple strategies. There seems to always be more than one way to make money on a project. It is just choosing which one you want to do most.

Shannon:
The last question of the chapter is, what type of legacy do you want to leave?

Steve:
I want to leave a legacy that promotes growth, that promotes free thinking, that promotes the ability for not only my kids but others to be able to go out and to make it on their own. For them to not have their futures and what they do in life be determined by somebody else. And that's fine, if individuals work for others. We need the doctors, the attorneys, the school teachers. You need all of those individuals. But we can also promote that people go out and do things on their own. Create wealth and cash flow on the side. Create the ability to be able to live life on their terms and not be determined by others.

One of my sons loves the theater. But he said to me, 'Dad, I know that the theater will not give me the lifestyle that I want. Therefore, I would like you to help me do real estate investing so that I can get the cash flow, so I can do the thing that I love but be able to live the lifestyle that I want.'

And to see that legacy starting with my children, and the individuals that we've been able to work with, brings me great joy and excitement for life and for the future, to be able to go out and to help and strengthen and empower those around me.

Scott O'Shaughnessy

Scott O'Shaughnessy was born in OC (Orange County, California) but considers himself a Pacific Northwest native, having grown up and spent most of his life there. Scott is a husband, father, 26-year retired Navy veteran, and real estate investor with 20+ years' experience. Scott and his wife, Anna, began their investing career in 1995 when they bought a duplex with Scott's VA benefits. Instantly realizing the power of cash flow, Scott was hooked. Armed with an MBA in project management and a background in operations and maintenance, Scott and Anna would "House Hack" at each new duty station. They still do this today.

Once Scott retired in 2014, he pursued real estate, helped Anna grow her catering business, Crescent Moon Catering, and as assisted others with a passion. Retiring from one great community, he actively sought out another to apply his skills and knowledge to. His company is known as Goat Locker Real Estate, as a homage to his days as a Navy Chief. He is recognized as a leader in his local community for real estate information and has contributed to several pod casts, leads a highly successful study group, and is now a first-time author. All the while he has been helping his friends and former shipmates learn the power and benefits of positive cash flow and what it can do for them and their families' legacies.

Shannon:

Scott, according to Forbes magazine, real estate is one of the top three ways that people become wealthy. As a real estate expert, why do you feel this is the case?

Scott:

Well honestly, I think it's for the multiple benefits that it provides when somebody's doing an investment. You've got the added benefit of cash flow. It's got the opportunity to make massive piles of money, as we call it, and also passive income along with appreciation that's thrown in there, and the various different ways.

It's not just one single focus investment strategy in a single product, so to speak; you get multiple ways to grow and to increase your wealth while doing everything else.

Shannon:

If someone was going to get started in real estate, what would you recommend that they do first?

Scott:

I love this question; I get asked this a lot. I always tell everybody that you've got to get a good education because everybody knows you can make a lot of money in real estate, but you also can lose it if you don't know what you're doing, and then you're out of the game. Or you get upset and say, 'This stuff doesn't really work.' So, first thing you do, you've got to get yourself a good education.

Shannon:

What inspired you to get into real estate?

Scott:

I don't really know. The wife always says that since she's known me I've had a big bug about real estate, maybe because of my parents in growing up, we never really owned our own place and kind of bounced around from rental to rental to rental. And the few times that we actually did find a place, it didn't really work out. So maybe it was just the initial drive to have a place of my own. And then I realized what it could do for me financially and for my family. And that's kind of how we got started.

Shannon:
How has your education in real estate changed the way that you invest?

Scott:
I think what it's done is allowed me to focus and learn exactly what my investment strategy is, or what my investor DNA is, as J. Massey puts it. It accounts for me becoming very focused and centralized on being a cash flow guy. That's how I invest, and that's how I look at things.

And that's how, when I do my analytics on everything, I ask what the cash flow is going to be on the property. How is it going to work? And how is that going to benefit my investors?

So, the education has been very beneficial. Because, prior to that, it was just kind of swinging it, just taking a guess out there and figuring out if it makes sense or not, from a purely financial point of view, not taking the rest of everything else into account.

Shannon:
What is cash flow, and why should it be such an important focus of your business?

Scott:
Well cash flow is the ability of a property to make you money once all your bills, all the debts, the note servicing and everything else is done and paid off. And for me, at the stage I'm at in my life with my family and everything else, it allows us to focus on the month to month in bringing stuff in.

And as you build those little nuggets of cash flow along the way, they add up to a pretty consistent income, so that way you don't have to go out and work for the W-2, or you can take your time to take a trip to Europe for three weeks and know that money's still coming in. So, it allows you to build that passive business along the way that most people don't realize and don't think about until they wake up one day and it's like, 'Hey, we're doing pretty good here.'

Shannon:
If you're starting with little money or poor credit, what are some strategies to get into real estate?

Scott:

Well one of the ones I like is the partnering up with somebody to learn from, so possibly doing a joint venture with them to where you're putting your time and your relationships in to be able to start earning that money and everything else.

Or, once again, using your knowledge, that other currency, be able to go through and learn how to wholesale properties or maybe do some lease options. There are some entry-level ways to get in there until you can start making sufficient amounts of cash. You can go out and start pulling down your own deals and even making bigger deals after that. So, you just start small and work your way up.

Shannon:

How have mentors in your real estate investing helped you navigate potential pitfalls?

Scott:

It's just learning and being able to ask questions, to go back to them and say, 'Hey, what do you think of this? Can you go look at this project with me? Can run the numbers with me?' And it's saved us from investing in some really bad deals that initially looked pretty good on paper. But then you go out and you walk the property, or you really take a look at the analytics, and they ask, 'Hey, did you guys think about this, or what about that?' And once you sit down and take a look at everything, you realize that it's not really a good deal at all.

Shannon:

In your business, how do you help other people learn more about real estate?

Scott:

Well one of the nice things and the benefits I get to do with our local group is I facilitate our study groups for the beginner investors. And so, it allows me to kind of pay it forward or pay it back to all those people who helped me get started in doing this. So, the beginners can learn and, once again, ask questions, and now I get to ask them 'What about this and what about that? And have you gone through everything?'

And it's nice to see that light bulb go off, to see that progression of somebody coming in who's bright-eyed, bushy-tailed thinking they're going to set the world on fire, make tons of money, and then really knuckle down and start doing something. And they get their first project, and it's successful. It's a good reward to see that.

Shannon:
What do you think the number-one mistake an individual makes when buying their first investment property?

Scott:
Oh, they paid too much for it, right off the bat. They go through and they buy it retail. They get together with the realtor, who doesn't necessarily understand investing strategies, but they understand the retail market. And so, they think that, 'Hey, if I pay 10 percent below market value, then I've got a good deal. I've made 10 percent in equity.' And, yeah, you may have, but it doesn't necessarily mean you are cash flowing the amount that you potentially could for the property.

Shannon:
Is real estate investing success dependent on a strong economy?

Scott:
No, not at all. You can make money if the market goes up and if the market goes down. Once again, it's knowing your different strategies and being able to get creative sometimes, because that's where you make your money. You can help people out, whether the economy's strong or if another great recession comes along.

Shannon:
Explain to me one example of a good process to use in a strong economy.

Scott:
I would say probably the best one is to work with people who are looking for a good cash flow and can raise private funds. And use that, use other people's money, to help buy your properties. So, you get in and get them, and teach them about appreciation, and all the benefits they have in it, and what it can do tax-wise, and strategies. So, you can use their money to help build your real estate portfolio.

And at the same time, they help increase their retirement funds. And they have it all secured by something stable like real estate, not in stocks and bonds that even in a good economy can be very volatile.

I mean, take a look at MCI, Enron, a lot of those guys who were great for the longest time and then, overnight, just disappeared.

Shannon:

How about in a down economy, what's a good strategy for making money in a weak economy?

Scott:

Well there's a couple of different ones. Short sales are obviously the first ones that come to mind because a lot of times in a down economy houses will either flat line or people, will have to move and they need to sell their property. But they can't get what they owe on it, so they're kind of upside down.

Shannon:

When doing a short sale, is there something that you should really anticipate? And how long do they take from beginning to end?

Scott:

I will tell you, I've never successfully done a short sale. The process takes so long. Or at least with the few that I've tried to do it's been six to nine months before ever actually getting anything from the bank.

And as one of my mentors Brian Meara told me, 'One of the hardest parts is it's got to be direct from the homeowner to the bank to be able to make it successful.' And he used to teach this around the country. That's something I've never been able to do.

So, I think that's probably the hardest part, making sure that you're the main guy from the homeowner to the bank. And I would say be prepared for a long time, it could be six months, nine months, or a year.

Shannon:

How can an individual benefit from a lease option?

Scott:

Well that question depends on where you stand as an individual. If you're the potential homeowner who doesn't have good credit, say you're self-employed, it allows you to get into a house, gives you the option to be able to purchase it, get started in building some equity, and get into a nice place without having to go through traditional financing.

Same thing if you're the owner. It allows you to get a good, quality person in there, one who has the potential to buy it down the road. And it gives you a higher-quality tenant because they're thinking, 'Hey, I got to purchase this place. I'm going to take care of it. I got to make sure it's in good shape, because one of these days, I'm going to own this place.'

Shannon:

If someone wanted to invest in multifamily dwellings, what do they need to know?

Scott:

A higher financial literacy. You got to understand how your property's cash flow per unit, not necessarily just a single one, and then what it's going to cost to actually manage and maintain the whole place as well. Also, you need to understand how to comp it because it's not the same as a single-family residence.

So that's a little bit of the minor differences of being there. And then you're down to just working the numbers and understanding what type of apartment building you're looking at. What type of neighborhood is that? And that part is kind of similar to a single-family residence.

Shannon:

When you began your real estate investing career, did you establish your team to help you be successful or did you go at it on your own?

Scott:

I went at it on my own. And that's the complete and wrong way to do it. I'm a retired Navy officer, and I bought my first duplex using my VA loan benefits. And basically, the wife and I would invest every time we got transferred. I've kind of figured out and found out afterwards, and got a little bit better educated, that we were just really lucky in what we did.

So, I would tell everybody to get their team together as they're getting their education, so that way when they're ready to strike, they're ready to go. I went about it kind of the back-end way, and I think that definitely slowed the progress of where we got to go and what we got to do.

Shannon:
Most millionaires and billionaires have investments in commercial real estate. Why do you think that is?

Scott:
It's just a numbers game, plain and simple. One, it allows them to have kind of a tax haven for their money, where to put it and get it to work for them. But when you're dealing with that number of zeros, when you're dealing in multimillion dollar properties, a couple hundred thousand makes a big difference in the actual payoff. So, if you got the cash, you might as well step up and play with the big boys.

Shannon:
What advice would you give to someone who is allowing fear to hold them back from starting in real estate investing?

Scott:
Two things. Once again, it all comes back to education. The more knowledgeable you are, the less fear you're going to have. Second, fear's a good thing. It keeps you from doing something irrational and getting yourself in trouble. And then third, partner with somebody.

That's the beauty and benefit of having a good community around you to support you and help you learn, as they'll help guide you through the pitfalls that they've had before, and it allows you to go ahead and kind of minimize that fear. It still should be there, right, but make it a little less.

Shannon:
So, the last question of the chapter is, for some people, the easiest and for some people the hardest: What type of legacy do you want to leave?

Scott:
That is, wow, I guess that's the question, huh? I'd have to say, I have to take a play out of Garrett Gunderson's book, What Would the Rockefellers Do? Having learned some of his strategies, I want my family, down the road, to be able to say, 'Scott was the guy who established us and got us going, and we took it from there.'

I've got nothing from my parents, grandparents, or great-grandparents, other than maybe a couple of pieces of furniture, because nobody in my family took the time to learn about their financial education. No one knew how to set up a trust, how to establish a good, residual, passive income for down the road, and then make it last, not just a big inheritance and it's gone. So that's what I've got to do.

Derrick & Paula Porter

Derrick and Paula Porter are military veterans who both grew up in the Midwest. They had different career paths until fate (and the military) brought them together in 2008. Derrick and Paula have six children and one grandchild, and one of their primary goals is to create a lasting legacy through real estate investing.

Paula's customer service and sales experience is an invaluable asset for their company's growth. While working as a sales representative in the communications industry, she regularly exceeded her sales goals and achieved tremendous growth in her market.

Derrick has more than 20 years of experience in electronic maintenance and repair, including aviation, copiers and fax machines, printing presses, arcade games, food processing, and nuclear power. He served in the U.S. Marine Corps for 6 years and for the past 10 years has served in the U.S. Navy Reserves as part of a construction unit.

They now share a vision of helping others become successful entrepreneurs through real estate investing. It was during a deployment in Afghanistan that Derrick, while talking with a fellow service member, learned of a real estate investing education platform that set them on a path to becoming successful real estate investors.

By applying knowledge gained through education, Derrick and Paula have partnered with other investors to put 29 units under contract using little of their own credit and no out of pocket money.

Shannon:
According to Forbes magazine, real estate is one of the top three ways people become wealthy. As a real estate expert, why do you feel this is the case?

Derrick:
Because people will always need shelter...clean, safe, affordable housing. Real estate historically tends to increase in value. It provides great tax advantages.

Shannon:
What inspired you to get into real estate?

Derrick:
I was speaking with a fellow service member when I was deployed to Afghanistan in 2014 about how I was kind of tired of being away from home, living paycheck to paycheck, and spending 50 to 80 hours a week dealing with my job. He mentioned having some rental properties which provided him with passive income. It peaked my interest as a way to be able to create income and wealth without having to be away from my family all the time.

Shannon:
When you got started in real estate, what was one of the biggest pieces of advice that he gave you?

Derrick:
Learn the basics and find like-minded individuals who are willing to discuss ideas, share experiences, evaluate potential deals, and run numbers with you. Having someone else to point out the things that you are forgetting or errors that you have made in the evaluation process can save you a ton of money and frustration.

Shannon:
How do you feel that mentors in your real estate investing have helped you navigate some potential pitfalls?

Derrick:
Mentors have definitely helped; you just don't always think of all the details. You don't think of checking into all the little nuances that

might come up, like even how the utilities are split up amongst a building. And how that can affect whether you can actually charge each unit individually. Or if you have to just, as a landlord, cover the entire cost. You know, something like that would have never occurred to me to consider.

Shannon:

If someone wanted to invest in multi-family dwellings, what do you feel is one of the most important things that they should know?

Derrick:

With multi-family dwellings, I think they should really know how to manage a property or locate a good property manager to manage it for them. That seems to be the biggest issue amongst multi-family dwellings is finding a good property manager to keep all your units full and properly maintained.

Shannon:

When you are looking at multi-family units, what is your goal? I know 100 percent is the goal for keeping them rented, but in all reality, what would be a realistic expectation where you could still remain profitable?

Derrick:

That will vary by market. Of course you want the highest occupancy possible. I make it a goal to always be at 90 percent occupancy or better. If it drops below 90 percent, then it may be time to evaluate the market rents, your advertising methods, the trends in the neighborhoods, and some possible incentives you can provide.

Shannon:

What is one of the top real estate strategies that you have learned?

Derrick:

I like the buy and hold strategy because I like the passive income. Having and creating long-term wealth by holding on to the property. Taking advantage of the tax benefits, as well as gaining value as the property appreciates. Mostly I just like the passive income.

Shannon:

Explain to me, how does real estate allow you to earn massive and passive income?

Derrick:

The massive income is going to be more with a fix and flip or some sort of buy low, sell high deal where you can profit potentially tens of thousands of dollars off of one transaction. Where with passive income, you're looking at getting a good net operating income every month. To build a portfolio to meet whatever your monthly goals are.

If you wanted $10,000 a month, you just must do the math. How many doors, how many units, do you need in order to get to that number? And it gives you a good benchmark for gaining that passive income.

Shannon:

What is cash flow and why should it be such an important focus of your business?

Derrick:

Cash flow is the money that's left over after you've paid all the bills. If you don't have any cash flow, then you're just breaking even. That doesn't leave any money to go out and continue to build your portfolio, grow your net worth, and live the life you want to live. If all you're doing is breaking even, then you will likely need another source of income to provide for your family or to have anything extra like being able to take vacations.

Shannon:

When doing a fix and flip, what do you want to look out for?

Derrick:

I would say with a fix and flip, just trying to look out for the unexpected. Trying to be as prepared as possible for example, when we tear down this wall, are we going to find plumbing issues or structural issues. Maybe it looks okay while the dry wall's up. But the more you get into it, the more repairs you find are needed. Just being as thorough as possible whenever you're inspecting the property so you get the most accurate repair costs.

Shannon:

Do you think that when you're doing a buy and hold, you would look out for those same things?

Derrick:

Most definitely. You want to make sure that just because it's cash flowing on paper, the way it sits doesn't mean that a previous owner has taken care of it properly. You might end up losing all of your cash flow for the first three or four months or more fixing all of the deferred maintenance.

Shannon:

What is deferred maintenance?

Derrick:

Maybe they haven't kept up with the roof, you know the 30-year roof that's been on there for 40 years. Maybe they have not painted for 10 years and all the paint's peeling off of it. Or they left the carpet in there for longer than they should. They were just deferring their costs by not doing the regular upkeep.

Shannon:

Thank you, that makes sense. In your business, how do you help other people learn more about real estate?

Derrick:

Paula wants to answer this one.

Paula:

I got this one. We have found that what we are learning is so powerful and inspiring to others, that Derrick and I have started doing presentations in the Milwaukee market and growing the community of real estate investors up in that area. We bring in guest speakers and successful real estate investors to share on a regular basis what they have learned in doing deals, what they are currently doing, and what other successes they have had since becoming educated in real estate.

We have built a very strong real estate community in the Milwaukee area. July 18th will be our one year anniversary and it has grown leaps and bounds. The enthusiasm, the excitement, the property tours we're starting to do—everything has really gained attention, not only in Milwaukee, but around the country. We're excited to see how it will grow even more in the future.

Shannon:
How has your education in real estate changed the way that you invest?

Derrick:
Having the education gives you more knowledge, more confidence to be able to pursue deals that you would typically think you're not capable of doing. A lot of people think, 'well there's no way I can invest in real estate because I don't have any money or credit.' But once you become educated, you come to realize that it doesn't have to be your money or credit to invest in real estate.

You learn a lot of different strategies, different ways to do things. Most people are used to the retail side of things. Example: I want to buy a house. I have to use my credit, I have to go to the bank or use my life savings to make that happen. And that's the way I believe that most people view trying to invest in anything.

Shannon:
If you're starting with very little money or poor credit, what are some of the strategies to get into real estate?

Derrick:
Networking with other investors. Once you are educated and you have the knowledge, you know how to speak to other investors and you know how to find good deals. When other investors see that quality in you, that's when they are confident to invest in your deal. You can also partner with other members of a community of investors. You can learn how to approach sellers to do seller financing instead of having to go to a bank to use your credit.

Or doing maybe just a 'subject to' type of deal where you just take over their mortgage payments. There's a lot of different strategies for it. Once you become educated and learn how to speak with sellers and buyers both, it really increases your odds of being able to complete deals without using any of your own money or credit.

Shannon:
Where do you typically find these people to network with? Where do you find a seller to even approach about doing a seller finance or a subject to?

Derrick:
Well you can of course you can find stuff just in a listing. For sale by owner signs, or websites, word of mouth. As you become more knowledgeable, more versed and complete more deals, people will tell their friends: 'Hey, this person was able to help me out when I was in this situation, why don't you give them a call?'

Really being educated and being able to speak in the right terms will help you grow leaps and bounds.

Shannon:
Paula, how has real estate changed your life?

Paula:
It's really opened a lot of windows for us. We have six kids and a grandbaby. We see the long-term benefit of investing in real estate. You know it's growing a legacy from generation to generation. Our kids are very much involved in what we do. They help us a lot whether they go to work on a fix and flip or coming up to the Milwaukee office, checking people in, cleaning or just visiting with guests. It's teaching our kids great work ethics and morals, while building their confidence.

That is something that is hard to do on a regular basis when you work a W2 job. You can't take your kids to work with you and have them see what you do every single day. When you're involved in real estate investing, they can see because you get to work from home. I get say to them, 'Hey listen, this is what we're going to do on the fix and flip today, are you guys in?' And they usually get excited and say, 'Yes!' They get to see a little bit of that creativity and the different possibilities in fix and flips or a multi-family unit.

It's great passing that on to your kids and showing them how it's just going to grow. Then, when they get to that age where they're like, 'Oh, what do we want to do with our life,' they remember, 'Hey, we can stay home and we can create our own time. Let's do real estate investing.' They can see the passive income just coming in every month. And realize they don't have to sit behind a desk for the next 40 years.

That's been a great eye opener for me and having our kids involved in what we do in real estate investing has been a blessing.

Shannon:
Thank you. Derrick, same question to you. How has real estate changed your life, if you have anything to add to what Paula just said.

Derrick:
For me it has created a light at the end of the tunnel sooner than I would have thought. I planned on working until I was 57 or 60. I just figured that's what I had to do, that's how you're brought up. And I think most Americans are brought up that way. You have to go to school, go to college, get good grades so you can get a good job, so you can have this life that you want.

But then you get the good job and they want you to work 50, 60, 70 hours a week. And that doesn't leave a whole lot of time for living your life. There have been times in my life that I have worked three or four jobs to make ends meet. Now I'm in the position that I have a good job and a member of the military reserve, so my time is very valuable.
And to be able to see into the not-so-far future, I can leave my job and have more time with my family. That is huge for me.

Shannon:
Do you feel that real estate investing success is dependent on a strong economy?

Derrick:
No, real estate investors make money no matter how the economy doing. It's a matter of knowing your markets, knowing when to buy, when to sell, and when to hold onto it. For example, if there is a down economy, maybe you just want to hold onto it until the economy recovers. You're still collecting rent from those properties, so you will still be making money.

If you have positioned yourself well enough, you may even be able to help some of those people out by re-negotiating their rent a little bit. The knowledge that you can learn through education and through networking with other investors is priceless. You can learn how to make money through all the ups and downs of the economy.

Shannon:

Since you don't feel that real estate investing is dependent on a strong economy, why do you think most people fail at real estate?

Derrick:

A lot of it is lack of knowledge, education, and/or attitude. A lot of people think they want to be a landlord, but then they start dealing with all the headaches that come along with being a landlord, so they decide it really isn't for them. They get tired of getting phone calls at three in the morning every time the fire alarm goes off at their apartment building, or the toilet needs to be fixed, or even trying to collect rent every month.

Maybe they think they're going to make money on their fix and flip. They don't have the necessary knowledge to realize that their repair costs were going to be thousands more because of electrical/pumping issues, pests, mold, etc. And they end up losing money on it. And let's face it, nobody likes to lose money. If you go into a deal thinking you're going to come out ahead $20,000 or $30,000 and instead you end up negative $5000 out of pocket, that's going to deter a lot of people from ever trying it again.

Shannon:

Why do you think the people who succeed continue to have success? What's their secret?

Paula:

I think a huge secret to being successful in real estate is to always have an open mind. Always be willing to learn and have an open mind. Whether it's from reading a book, surrounding yourself with positive people, observing, you always have to continue to grow. Real estate is an ever-changing market and you have to learn to change with it.

I've talked to people who have been in real estate for 20 years and they don't understand why they were so successful 20 years ago and now they're having problems. It's because they're not changing with the times, so you have to not only be open minded to knowledge, but you have to be open minded to changing with the economy, with time and everything that goes along with that.

Shannon:

How do you feel that learning multiple investment strategies protects and accelerates your investing success?

Derrick:

The more strategies you educate yourself with and get good at, the more opportunities will present themselves to be able to make money. If you focus in on only one strategy, maybe it will work great in one market but completely be unsuccessful in another. What happens if the economy turns, there's a housing shortage or something changes with just the demographics" All of a sudden, your one strategy is no longer working and your business comes to a screeching halt because you realize you don't have any other strategies to apply.

Shannon:

How can an individual benefit from a lease option?

Derrick:

With a lease option you can benefit by being able to get what I'd say is a chunk of money upfront. Also you get passive income for a length of time. You can set an option fee to receive $10,000. Maybe you had to do a little bit of rehab to that property, you end up getting rehab costs back up front. Plus you still have the monthly passive income from the monthly lease payments.

Shannon:

What type of legacy do you want to leave?

Paula:

Derrick and I have talked about this. We want to leave a legacy that you can be successful and not have to work the typical W2 job. We want our kids to have the knowledge we didn't have. We want them to be happy and successful.

A lot of people that work every single day, get up to fight traffic, fight the clock, and miss valuable family time. We want our kids to be able to have the freedom that we never had.

We were never taught growing up to think freely. Like Derrick said earlier, we are brought up thinking you have to go to high school to get good grades so you can get into a good college. Then graduate and get your diploma and spend the majority of your adult life paying off loans and being unhappy with your job.

I want our children to be able to do what they want with their time instead of somebody else telling them. Not be slaves in the corporate world.

Even on weekends, you know everybody dreads Mondays, and we don't want our kids to dread any day. Every day's going to be a pay-day Friday to them. They can do what they want and that's what we want to do as a legacy. I'm going to let Derrick continue...

Derrick:
Besides just leaving the legacy for our kids, we want to create a legacy that's lasting generation to generation to generation. We want our kids to have the knowledge to continue to create and build the legacy, pass it on to their kids and their grandkids and to just create wealth that goes for many generations. And to also leave a portion of that legacy to not just our family but also help others.

Through real estate, we see how we can create the legacy of our families, while still creating portfolios that the cash flow promotes and can go to a charity of your choice. You can leave the whole portfolio to a charity if you so desire. It's the knowledge we've seen, that's the legacy. It's keeping the knowledge growing for generations so that the wealth creation and maintaining that wealth can continue on to our great great great grandkids.

Jessyka Scala

Jessyka Scala spent most of her young life in Massachusetts where she attended high school and college. She grew up on the south coast of Puerto Rico in the small town of Las Ochenta in the city of Salinas. During her simple beginnings as a loving sister to four brothers, she was studious and friendly with a strong character; she was always willing to help others that helped her become the social network force she is today. She went on to be a single mother to daughter Jessie and late son Carlos. She always worked hard at everything she did and became the best parent she could to her children. Later in life, she became a mother to two adoptive children, daughter Sachi and son Dominic, who are two of the biggest blessings in her life. In 2011, she relocated to Illinois and married husband Robert Scala. It was then that she decided to do more for her family, starting as an entrepreneur and then venturing into real estate investing. She likes to spend time with her family and visit her grandkids Jon Preston and Ella-Grace in Florida as often as possible. Her goal is to inspire and help other women to never give up and to strive for success. She is a recipient of the prestigious Vincent Ardelean Service Cup.

Shannon:
What inspired you to get into real estate?

Jessyka:
For me, I started working in corporate America and never felt I was earning enough or the amount of money that I was worth. I began to look for alternate ways to generate income. I'd always wanted to start my own business and was interested how much money was being made in real estate investing.

One of the people who inspired me is a family member and my mentor, and she just recently retired after working 40 years for the government. I saw all the changes in her life, how she was approaching life as an entrepreneur, as a real estate investor, and how she was utilizing money whether it was in capital or whether it was IRAs to succeed. And investing, not just for herself and her husband, but for her entire family.

Shannon:
How have mentors in your real estate investing helped you to navigate potential pitfalls?

Jessyka:
Learning from the experiences of your mentors is huge and under-utilized. You learn more from the mistakes that are made, but no one said that they must be your mistakes. One of the advantages is that you are learning from someone else's mistakes and avoid making them.

Shannon:
If someone was going to get started in real estate, what would you recommend they do first?

Jessyka:
Knowledge is not only powerful, it's profitable, so I can't emphasize enough for people to actually get educated and start learning the basics: business development, how to turn their business into a tax deduction machine, and how to hang on until their income is down-rated. Learn how to properly handle the money generated and protect your assets. Learn creative financing and how not to use their own money.

Shannon:
What is one of the top real estate strategies that you have learned?

Jessyka:
IRAs are a great way to raise money to fund investments. It is a win for both of us. For the investor who found themselves in this position, they have the opportunity to earn substantially more income than letting it just sit in additional account. And for the buyer, this means that no out of pocket money is needed, which is a beautiful thing.

Shannon:
What are some creative ways to acquire a property?

Jessyka:
Seller financing, IRAs, but I think one of my favorites is purchasing real estate inside an HSA, a health savings account. With the cost of health insurance increasing, being it's a profit earned, or your cash flow to cover your health cap cost, and using it as deductions in your tax returns. It also is another way to grow a tax-free retirement account.

Shannon:
It's interesting that you are helping people use their HSAs because it seems like those accounts are really under-utilized.

Jessyka:
Absolutely.

Shannon:
Is this something that a mentor helped you learn or is this something that you thought of on your own?

Jessyka:
I didn't think of it on my own. It's part of getting all of the information from education that I'm obtaining, from networking with the right people, with a good community of investors so you get to see what works for other people, and what doesn't work for other people.

Shannon:
In your business, how do you help other people learn about real estate?

Jessyka:

I don't share legal details. It doesn't necessarily have to be mine, it can be from my community or team. I can take them to property tours where they can see first-hand how properties are acquired and re-habbed. And that process is also designed to sell in different types of neighborhoods, and how the projected AIV is figured.

Shannon:

What do you think is the number one mistake an individual makes when buying their first investment property?

Jessyka:

Not analyzing the deal. You have to have good numbers and allow enough money for the unexpected, what we call the 10 percent oops factor. Anything can go wrong, whether it's structural or otherwise, so always leave that 10 percent oops factor. A lot of investors have an issue with that. Or another issue that I see is not covering all the ba-ses when it comes to their team, you know, a private manager, a man-ager that is in charge of the documents, a negotiator. Every single member that you hire for that team, you need all those things in place.

Shannon:

What advice would you give to someone who is allowing fear to hold them back from starting their real estate investing?

Jessyka:

Fear is a good thing. It keeps us honest. It shows caution and keeps you from jumping and making rash decisions potentially leading to expensive mistakes. I also explain that their current situation will stay as it is until they make the jump and get started.

Shannon:

Do you feel that real estate investing success is dependent on a strong economy?

Jessyka:

No, as a matter of fact, you can purchase deeply discounted real es-tate in a weak economy. You can increase profits and your cash flow, depending on the strategies you use. To go back to 2007 and 2008 when there was the crash, the more educated investors were the ones making the money, and everybody else was looking for a way out.

Shannon:
What is cash flow and why should it be such an important focus of your business?

Jessyka:
Cash flow is cash coming in and out. Without cash flow you can't invest, you can't earn properties. Simply put, it is what's left over from the rental income when the expenses are paid off each month. If there is a surplus, that is a positive cash flow. If there is a deficit, that is a negative cash flow. It allows you to earn a steady income while waiting for the other strategies that you are using to come in maybe every six or so months. Let's say you are renting a property for $1,200; that's great monthly cash flow, but at the end of the day, if what you are earning is not the same amount of money that you need to spend, that's negative cash flow.

Shannon:
How does real estate allow you to earn massive income and passive income?

Jessyka:
Owning multiple rentals can be as easy as buying one a year. You need to make sure that rentals alone generate positive cash, and figure out the property management so that you can leverage your time to look for turnkey properties. There are other options once you start acquiring multiple properties, such as taking out low-interest loans on the equity to either rehab and help increase the value, allowing you to increase the rent, or just sell it for a profit.

Shannon:
What is one thing that you should look out for when you are looking for a fix and flip?

Jessyka:
The first thing I see is the condition. You have to make sure that all the numbers are going to be played the right way. You know off-hand, without having to run those numbers, what is going to be the

profit margin for you, what it's going to cost you, and all the other possible things that may be going on with that particular property, whether it's in the structure of the property, the back yard, I mean, everything. And sometimes I feel like you kind of have to guess before investing in this particular property just by looking at it.

Shannon:
What is the first thing you look for when you are purchasing a rental property?

Jessyka:
When I'm looking through a rental property, the first thing that I look for is all the factors. There are a lot of misconceptions. People don't get into those kinds of properties because of who they have to deal with. There are a lot of factors involved with fixing and flipping, such as fixing it and selling it, but with rentals, there is a little bit more to it. You need to find property management, and you need to be sure of the source of the income that it's going to generate for you, especially if it's a property that has multiple units. The individuals who are renting have their own issues, their own factors for why they are renting. So buying and knowing all this concerning renting to others, you need to know there are a lot of difficulties for you as well.

Shannon:
If someone wanted to invest in multi-family dwellings, what do they need to know?

Jessyka:
Multi-family is not for everybody. It takes a different kind of investor, an investor that is seasoned, an investor who has proper funding in case a lot of things go wrong. You need funding to have other people taking care of that property for you because you can't constantly be there. It's going to take a lot of people backing you up that you can look to and get advice. It is very different than a one-unit residential home.

Shannon:
How can an individual benefit from a lease option?

Jessyka:

You pay an option fee for the right to buy later within a certain time frame or don't buy if you choose not to. Give yourself one to two years to project the value (sweet spot) for a single property and five to ten years for commercial property.

Shannon:

How has real estate changed your life?

Jessyka:

It has changed the way I look at spending money. Instead of spending money just to own things, I look at what my ROI will be. It has taught me the power of passive income and leveraging time.

Shannon:

Why do you think people succeed in real estate?

Jessyka:

Educated real estate investors succeed by gaining a wide range of knowledge in different strategies and being prepared for the unexpected. They know how to have information at their disposal, have the skill to negotiate deals for the market value, use skilled professionals, and never enter into a deal without three or more exit strategies.

Shannon:

In your real estate investing career, are you currently looking to do fix and flips, or buy and holds, or wholesale?

Jessyka:

Fix and flip—as long as I keep the emotion out. Whatever property I want to fix, flip, and then just sell it, the numbers have to guide me. Fix and flip is for me.

Shannon:

Why do you need to keep the emotions out?

Jessyka:

I was just observing a recent deal that went sour. And the reason why that deal went sour was because, first of all, the person who was trying to bring this to the table was doing this for two kids who had acquired property. That property had an emotional attachment to the person bringing up the deal, so when certain things were not going the way they should have been, well, though you always want to look out for your family, you have to do it in a way that the outcome is selling off that property, whether it's a huge investment or a huge profit or not.

The person that brought the deal to the table had two sons, and the sons were attached because this would be their home. So, of course the person wants to sell the property for the highest amount of money in order to secure their sons' financial future. When it takes an emotional toll like that, doing it because it belongs to somebody that you know, or doing it because it's a property that you owned in the past, it doesn't really let you focus on what is possible and what is not.

Shannon:
What do you think is the number one mistake an individual makes when they're buying their first investment property?

Jessyka:
For me there's more than one mistake. But one of the most important ones that resonates with me is that they didn't pick the right property. Not only did they not pick the right property, they didn't have the specific team members that they needed to cover every part of the deal. If you don't feel like you have the right partner, nothing good is going to come from it. So it's a huge mistake.

Shannon:
What are some creative ways to acquire a property to fix and flip?

Jessyka:
There are many ways of finding homes. I think the question should be, is that a home that you want to invest in? A lot of investors always look for a huge amount of profit. They forget that part of investing and being a well-rounded investor is creating a portfolio. In that portfolio, you want different investments—you want the big investments, you want the little investments.

Shannon:
What is the legacy that you would like to leave behind?

Jessyka:

The legacy that I want to leave behind is that everything you put your mind to, you can achieve—you can succeed if you get proper education. You know, I come from a background where I was a single mother for many years, so I know the struggle of working really hard, and by working really hard, I lost a lot of time being with my older kids. I don't want to work hard, I want to work smarter. So now, with my two younger kids, I want to spend as much time as possible with them. I want to give them the time. I want to do great things with them and teach them that when you gain that work smarter knowledge, you pretty much set your own course. Nobody is setting a path for you. Going to college and getting an 8-5 job is not the only way; it doesn't matter what vocation you end up doing, there is always a way.

Riley Shock

Riley Shock has been married to his wife Emily for 12 years and he has two boys, which he says are his greatest joy and success. He has always been fascinated with business ownership because he believes that is where you can have true freedom. After serving a two-year mission for his church, he started a construction business which he operated for a few years with some partners. He then transitioned to financial planning for a couple years until he opened a CrossFit gym, which he owned for six years. He had to close the gym down, but that led him to his career in real estate. He is now a full-time real estate investor, and he loves it. What he loves most about investing in real estate is that it offers him the freedom he has always been seeking in business ownership. When Riley is not passionately working on his business, he is with his family on a boat or in the mountains. He enjoys riding his dirt bike, wakeboarding, rock climbing, skiing, and anything else that gets his adrenaline pumping.

Shannon:

According to Forbes magazine, real estate is one of the top three ways people become wealthy. As a real estate expert, why do you feel this is the case?

Riley:

I agree that real estate is one of the best ways to become wealthy. One reason is there is a lot of potential for income in real estate investments. And also, because real estate or shelter is one of our basic needs. Therefore, there will always be a need for homes and buildings.

Shannon:

What inspired you to get into real estate?

Riley:

In 2016 I was closing down a business that I had owned for six years, and a friend of mine was interested in investing money to open it back up. We met together, and I told her what the potential income was if she invested and she declined. I asked her why she didn't want to invest, and she said she could make more money doing real estate. That piqued my curiosity, and I asked her how I could get into real estate.

Shannon:

If someone wanted to get started in real estate, what would you recommend that they do first?

Riley:

My recommendation actually comes from the advice of a very wealthy man who I interviewed at one point. He told me, never start a business in an industry that you don't have education in or where you don't know what you're doing. So, I would recommend going and finding some good education so that you're not starting something that you have no idea what you're doing.

Shannon:

If someone wanted to get started in real estate, but had very little money or poor credit, what are some strategies that they could use?

Riley:

I actually started my real estate career with very poor credit and I had no money. There are multiple strategies that can be used. What I started doing is fixing and flipping houses. I did it by using other people's money. I found that there are people I know who would lend me money because I could help them get a better interest rate than they can typically get in the stock market. There are many ways to do it though. You could also wholesale properties, which is generally a fast and simple way to make money in real estate. There are very many ways to get into real estate without using any of your own money or credit.

Shannon:

I'd like to go back to wholesaling, but first I'd like to know, when you're doing a fix and flip, what is one thing that you look out for?

Riley:

I am mainly looking to see if the numbers work: Is it going to make me money? When I look at the numbers I also am very conservative with them. I want to know that when things don't go as planned I will still make money. Too many people fall in love with the property and they try to fudge the numbers to make it work. That mindset will eventually hurt them.

Shannon:

What is your best strategy for finding fix and flips?

Riley:

Well there are two ways I look for properties. The first is actually probably the one I've done the most: finding people who are losing their house to the bank. I like that strategy because I'm actually helping people out. I teach them some of the options they have and help them get into a better situation. Though most of the properties that I've found so far have come from networking with people.

Shannon:

Earlier you mentioned wholesaling, where you don't actually buy the property, but you put it under contract. Can you explain that to me? How would you make money doing that?

Riley:

The way wholesaling works is you find an investment property and you put it under contract to buy it. You then go out and find a buyer (whether it is an investor or future homeowner) and you assign the contract to that person for a fee. I have used this strategy and it is nice because it takes very little resources in terms of money and credit. I also have bought properties from wholesalers which is also nice because there is less time spent finding properties.

Shannon:

What is a short sale and how long do they usually take from beginning to end?

Riley:

A short sale is a strategy to acquire properties typically from people who are losing their house to a bank through a foreclosure. The goal is to get the homeowner to agree to sell you the house and to get the bank to authorize to sell you the house for less than is owed to them, rather than foreclose. It can take a long time to get a short sale. I've heard of it taking two weeks but sometimes it'll take over a year in order to get a property through a short sale strategy.

Shannon:

How does real estate allow you to earn massive and passive income?

Riley:

Real estate allows you to make massive money through buy and sell strategies. This is flipping homes, apartment complexes, land and commercial buildings. Generally, these strategies lead to high short-term profits or massive money. Massive money strategies can make you a lot of money quickly which is great but unlike the passive money strategies you usually don't make money when you're not working. Passive is what I really love because to get passive money you work once and then you continue to get paid indefinitely. You get paid when you are on vacation, when you are sick, when you are lazy, and even when you die. Passive money generally comes from rents and leases from apartments, house rentals, commercial land and buildings.

Shannon:

If someone wanted to invest in multi-family dwellings, what do they need to know?

Riley:

I would go back to what my wealthy friend told me. Don't do any business without getting educated first. With multi-family there is a lot of money to be made, and there is also a lot that can be lost. I do know that there is a lot of opportunity to make money in multi-family dwellings.

Shannon:

Do you feel that real estate investing success is dependent on a strong economy?

Riley:

I do not think that real estate success is dependent on a strong economy. There are different strategies you could use depending on the economy. What tends to happen is when the economy is strong it may be harder to find properties, but they will generally sell faster. Though if the economy isn't strong, you'd be able to find a lot of good deals on properties but then they don't sell as quickly. There is a trade-off whenever the economy changes, therefore your strategies need to change. Another great example of this is when the economy is strong the contractors are harder to find at a reasonable price, and when the economy dips then you have your pick of contractors. So, I think the key actually is to be well prepared and educated on what strategies you could use when the economy changes. I look forward to investing in real estate when the economy dips.

Shannon:

What strategy would you use in a weaker economy to obtain properties?

Riley:

In a weak economy there will be good deals on the MLS because there will be a shortage of buyers. I would still use some of the strategies that I use now like foreclosure lists because banks will likely be willing to do a short sale, and I like to work with families who are struggling financially, and I can really help them out.

Shannon:
When you began your real estate investing career, how important was it for you to establish a team to help you be successful?

Riley:
It was very important to establish a team. You can't do it all yourself. There is too much to do and your projects will just become drudgery. I have made this mistake in previous businesses, and I was always behind and tired and I started to hate it. Also, my team really is the key to my success. Having a team when I started also gave me confidence that when I found a house I had the resources to get it done. I have money guys to fund the projects, I have a crew to get it done, an agent to sell it, and a title agent to have closing put together. If you don't have the team you will likely not have the confidence to put a good deal under contract. Also, the team is what runs your system, and it is your system that creates the lifestyle and freedom that I believe we are all looking for.

Shannon:
How has real estate changed your life?

Riley:
Real estate changed my life in multiple big ways. I've always been entrepreneurial minded, and I've had a few businesses, and one thing that I found is real estate actually gave me the lifestyle I wanted. The reason I've always been in business is because I wanted the freedom and the lifestyle; I wanted to experience life in ways many people never get to. I mean, I wanted to be able to travel, spend time with my boys, and watch them grow and learn. My previous businesses didn't allow me to do that. They tied me down and made me very busy, and real estate has given me more freedom; it's given me the systems that I needed in order to make more money and have more time to spend with my family and be able to pursue the goals that I have. On top of all that, I have grown and learned a lot about people, and I get to work with and help people, which I love.

Shannon:
How has your education in real estate changed the way that you invest?

Riley:

My education has been huge for me. It gave me confidence to go start investing. I knew what I was talking about and had confidence when talking to people about real estate. People were asking me for advice which actually led to my first deal. It also helped me to be successful on my first deal in contrast to all the stories I hear of people who dabbled in real estate and lost their shorts. I have learned what separates the wealthy real estate investors from the average investors. I did do a real estate flip a decade before getting educated, and I made all the mistakes and made very little money. Between that and market crashes and fear, I wrote off investing in real estate. Now after getting myself educated I make plenty of money on my deals, I don't make those huge mistakes, and I look forward to a market crash with no fear.

Shannon:

What do you feel is the number one mistake an individual makes when buying their first investment property?

Riley:

They don't run their numbers right when they buy a house. They hope the house values will continue to go up rather than planning in case they don't. They underestimate their repair costs and don't leave a buffer. And then they try to save money by doing all the work themselves, so the project ends up taking longer than expected which costs them more money.

Shannon:

In your business, how do you help others learn more about real estate?

Riley:

What I do to help others learn more about real estate is I give them the same opportunities as my friend (who introduced me to real estate) did for me. I lead them to where they can get educated on how to become a real estate investor then I can be there to offer up some accountability and possibly some connections that can help them be successful.

Shannon:
How have mentors in your real estate investment team helped you navigate potential pitfalls?

Riley:
Well, I think a mentor is key to being successful, in real estate and in business. For me having a mentor has helped me be accountable for doing what I say I will do. Also, a mentor helps you to not make the expensive mistakes. When I found my first deal I went to my mentor and said, "I have run the numbers over and over will you look at them and make sure I am not going to lose my shorts?" My success in real estate has been in a large part from the help and guidance I received from my mentors.

Shannon:
What type of legacy do you want to leave?

Riley:
My legacy has less to do with business and real estate and more to do with my family and my friends. That's what is important to me. Real estate is just a tool for me to get what I want. I want to be around for my family and do fun things with them. I want to look back on my life and be pleased with the memories I created and who I created them with.

I would say that my legacy outside of my family and being a part of that would be that I want to make a difference in other people's lives. I want to see people accomplish their goals and their dreams. I want people to enjoy life and be happy.

For me, having no regrets and living my life is something that has driven me ever since I was in high school. I didn't want to be mediocre and just have a job. I wanted to experience life, I want to be there for my family. I have found that I really want that for other people. Many have lost the American dream. I would like to bring it back.

Glen Suerte

Glen Suerte has a dual Bachelor of Science Degree from the University of Illinois at Chicago in Finance and Information Decision Science. With over 17 years of experience in the information technology field as a business systems analyst and build coordinator, Glen brings planning, analytical, attention to detail, and support skills to all his projects. Glen established GLS LTE ENTERPRISES, LLC in April 2018 and acquired a fix and flip rehab project with an ARV of $250,000. Glen enjoys spending time with family and friends, meeting new people every day, traveling, running, working out, and giving a helping hand within the event/race Industry by providing general ops/logistics support.

Shannon:

According to Forbes magazine, real estate is one of the three main ways people become wealthy. As a real estate expert, why do you feel this is the case?

Glen:

I believe that real estate is a great way to earn passive income especially from rental properties and taking advantage of the tax strategies, especially when you own your own business. You will have the opportunity to obtain cash flow and earn profits if you consistently run your numbers correctly. My goal is to complete several fix and flips in a given year, and with the profit I make from them, I plan to buy rental units to earn that passive income. Learning different acquisition strategies will help build and secure long-term wealth with real estate.

Shannon:

What is one of the top real estate strategies you have learned?

Glen:

I've been learning a lot these past few months, getting myself educated, but the strategy that I've been looking into is an agreement for deed strategy.

Shannon:

What is an agreement for deed strategy, and how do you benefit from that?

Glen:

There are multiple strategies that I have learned through my education for controlling properties and the benefits of using the various acquisition strategies. For the agreement for deed strategy, you could provide a down payment (as little as possible) and make periodic payments to buy the property. You can have an articles of agreement for deed documented and prepared by your real estate attorney to include verbiage to allow the purchaser to rehab a property to build value in that investment and have the ability to lease the property to retrieve rental income.

Also, you should have a memorandum recorded to certify that the agreement for deed is documented, which provides that the seller agrees to sell, and the buyer agrees to purchase the property at a set purchase price.

Shannon:
Is that similar to a seller finance?

Glen:
It is similar to owner-seller financing. You can structure a seller-financed deal with an installment sale agreement or an articles of agreement for warranty deed or contract for deed where the seller holds the title to the property until the buyer pays for the property in full. It is an agreement between a real estate seller and buyer, under which the buyer agrees to pay to the seller the purchase price plus interest in installments over a set period of time. One should consult with their real estate attorney to prepare the necessary documents based on the deal being constructed.

Shannon:
How can an individual benefit from a lease option?

Glen:
Lease option can benefit the seller by relieving their monthly mortgage payments, possibly deferring /avoiding capital gains, or taking depreciation on their income taxes (one should consult with their accountant), and possibly have no management responsibilities to their properties going forward.

Shannon:
How does that benefit the real estate investor?

Glen:
You can structure an option into a deal. An option is a contract, paying an up front, non-refundable option consideration / premium (as little as possible) for the right to buy the property over a specific time. You would need a lease to pay for the use of the property. If you are going to lease a building, you would need to be able to rehab it and sublease it out to have the ability to gain income.

Shannon:
When doing a fix and flip what do you want to look out for?

Glen:

With a fix and flip strategy, you should always make sure that you've got the correct ARV (After Repair Value). It is critical to know the ARV which would be the selling price of a property. You would get the comps, or the CMA (comparable market analysis—a real estate agent can provide to you), within the market area and then work backwards by deducting the repair/rehab costs, the closing costs, holding costs, your profit (20 percent of the ARV or double your repair costs), financing costs, and any unexpected expenses between 3 percent to 5 percent of the ARV.

The difference between a flip, fix and flip, and a rehab is that a rehab can range from a simple redecoration of internal structures to a major redesign. As for a flip, you're basically purchasing a property at a discounted rate and then selling it for a profit. For a fix and flip, you may be performing minor repairs to the property, such as replacing windows, painting, installing cabinets, or installing new carpet and flooring. For a rehab, it can be more detailed than a flip or a fix and flip. You are basically performing major redesigns to the property, making improvements to existing structures such as moving bathrooms, knocking down walls to create an open space concept, or redoing the main electrical panel, just to name a few.

Shannon:

What is cash flow and why should it be such an important focus of your business?

Glen:

Cash flow by definition is the total amount of money being transferred into and out of a business in a month, especially as affecting liquidity. It is an important focus for my business to ensure that I have adequate cash reserves; I do not want to run out of money. My goal these next two years is to complete several fix and flips and with the cash flow profit that I make on those fix and flips, I plan to purchase rental units or utilize my cash flow on any repair costs that I need to rehab on the building.

Shannon:

When you were beginning your real estate investing career how important was it for you to build a team to be successful?

Glen:

It is very important. You basically need to build your A-Team. You should list down the following individuals when establishing your team, such as your mentor(s), real estate attorney, accountant, contractors, handyman, real estate agents, home inspectors, appraisers, bank/ loan specialists, title escrow officers, and other resources such as your learning or business partner, to name a few.

Shannon:

How have mentors in your real estate investing helped you navigate potential disasters?

Glen:

There are several mentors within our local real estate community that I reached out to have them provide me with their thoughts and feedback. It's always good to hear potential pitfalls that may occur as you need to be prepared to handle them appropriately and adapt accordingly.

One main pitfall that I have learned from a mentor is not doing your due diligence and not doing extensive research in finding comps to come up with an ARV, time on market, closing costs, and repair costs. You should also give a 5 percent additional buffer just in case something happens.

Shannon:

If you're starting with little money or poor credit what are some strategies to get into real estate?

Glen:

If you have poor credit you can get an initial assessment and have a credit repair performed. I would build relationships with people in your warm market, and then in the long run, one of your resources could potentially be a private money lender for you.

Shannon:

What is private money and how do I get people to lend it to me?

Glen:

By definition, a private money lender is a non-institutional (non-bank) individual or company that loans money, generally secured by a note and deed of trust, for the purpose of funding a real estate transaction. These are individuals looking to achieve higher returns on their cash and that you have a close relationship with, whether it's your family, your friends, or someone that you've known for several years. You can inform them about the opportunity to invest in real estate and how they would be able to get a much higher rate of return on their money if they were to invest in properties that you're investing in.

Shannon:
What's the number one mistake somebody makes when buying their first property?

Glen:
Probably overpaying, also falling in love in the property, or using the wrong strategy. It is vital to determine if your real estate investment will be profitable. You will need to run numbers to ensure your cost analysis calculation is correct to determine your initial offer price of the property. As I mentioned earlier, it is critical to know the ARV, which would be the selling price of the property, to make sure that you get the proper cost within the market area and then work backwards by deducting all of the costs, your profit, and any unexpected expenses associated to the property.

Shannon:
How does falling in love with a property, how is that a mistake? Shouldn't you love what you do?

Glen:
Yes, but if you get emotionally involved in your investment property you get emotionally attached; then you most likely will overspend in doing your rehab. You just got to make sure that the repairs you're doing within that market area coincide with the other properties within that comparable market.

Shannon:
Glen, what inspired you to get into real estate?

Glen:

I've always wanted to get into real estate but just did not have the time or money to really pursue it. I knew that real estate was the key to earning passive income and just a way to take advantage of the tax benefits. However, for the past 17+ years, I worked in corporate America as an IT business systems analyst / build coordinator. Based on the project scope, I would work between 60 to 80 hours a week, so I just never had the time to really pursue real estate.

Last year, I was informed that my job position was being terminated. Everything happens for a reason. This now gave me the opportunity to pursue my real estate investing and entrepreneur journey full time. I invested in myself in getting educated in real estate investing and joining a community of like-minded individuals who were willing to support each other to become successful entrepreneurs.

Shannon:

How has real estate changed your life?

Glen:

Since I decided to become a real estate investor, I enjoy learning something new every day. My interests in real estate have increased tremendously as I continue to educate myself by watching videos, reading books, networking, and building relationships with other like-minded individuals. My mindset has changed since becoming an entrepreneur and a business owner. I am more focused and have direction in reaching my goals. Real estate investing is the key to building secure, long-term wealth. And having the thought of being financially free gives me piece of mind.

Shannon:

How has your education in real estate changed the way you invest?

Glen:

The education has helped me understand the process of real estate investing from start to finish, whether it's finding and analyzing a property, creating and making an offer, consulting with my real estate attorney, or just doing my due diligence. Learning the foundations of real estate investing, as well as any advanced strategy courses that I've learned from experienced practitioner instructors, has given me the knowledge to ensure that I'm applying what I've learned on the field properly. By educating myself on a daily basis, it keeps me focused. It has forced me to clearly identify my short-term and long-term goals for my business. I am always learning and will always be a student.

Shannon:

In your business, how do you help other people learn more about real estate?

Glen:

I inform other people about our local real estate investor community; we meet up every week for study group discussions. We learn from each other and support one another on our entrepreneurship journey. Through the education program, I let others know how they can take advantage on the tax savings and understanding the concepts of asset protection when acquiring a property. The online classes teach us financial freedom through education and community. We learn the facets of real estate investing starting from business ownership while we build secure and long-term wealth. First, learning the foundations of real estate investing by understanding the tax and legal strategies, credit management, the marketing aspects of real estate, the mortgage acceleration strategy, and the creative ways to make deals leading up to the advance investor training whether it's wholesaling, lease options, buy and hold, as well as notes, tax deeds and liens, to name a few.

I also inform them of property tours within our community that are conducted by real estate investors. They are willing to let the community know how they got the property, how they funded it, and the details within their process.

Shannon:

What type of the legacy do you want to leave?

Glen:

I want to live life with a purpose. I want to let people know that I was able to help them during their challenging situations and that I made a difference in their lives. If I fail in my entrepreneurial journey I know that I'll be able to bounce back and learn from my mistakes. I want to be able to spend more time with my family and friends. My goal is to be financially free and to not always worry about not having enough money to support my family and friends.

Adam Sullivan

Adam Sullivan is a real estate investor who resides in the country in Grant, Idaho. He and his lovely bride Melanie, of nearly 23 years, have 5 wonderful daughters: Samantha, Taylor, Maggie, Kennedy, and Olivia. He has lived in Idaho for the past 12 years, and after living there is fond of saying he never before lived in a place without a curb and sidewalk. Having been raised a city boy all his life in Orem, Utah, and Las Vegas, Nevada, the last several years brought new interesting experiences as he learned how to raise chickens, pigs, and cows with his girls, and he also learned how to deal with country varmints like skunks, porcupines, and raccoons.

Adam has two bachelor's degrees. One in Business Administration from Utah Valley University and the other in Occupational Safety and Health from Columbia Southern University. He is also working towards his MBA. Over the last several years, he has spent hundreds of hours working with the Red Cross teaching first aid skills.

Adam worked in construction management and safety for over 20 years and then decided he needed to get serious about getting an education in real estate. He currently has two personal companies and is a partner in several others.

Shannon:

According to Forbes magazine, real estate is one of the top three ways people become wealthy. As a real estate expert, why do you feel this is the case?

Adam:

I think because real estate is out there, and it's available for everyone. There are some great ideas that people have, like Bill Gates and Jeff Bezos, that take some time. Their stuff is maybe a lot more specialized, but real estate is out there. Property, houses, apartments, it's available for everyone. So, most people who take the time to go out and get involved will be very successful. I think that's just a pretty basic concept, something that I didn't take advantage for a long time, but when I started to realize that there is a lot of money to be made in real estate, and if you have a good education and you're with the right people, you're almost guaranteed success in my opinion.

Shannon:

What inspired you to get into real estate?

Adam:

That's a great question; I had two inspirations. The first one is when I found a notebook that I had written about a month or two after I'd got married that had some goals, and the second one on there was 'Invest in real estate.' So, my first inspiration was written when I was 21, and for 23 years I never did anything. I looked at that notebook for a long time, and I thought 'Man, I have to do that, I need to do that.' Every year I thought, 'I really ought to do that.' And finally, when I was in my mid-40s, the second major inspiration was when I was in Home Depot, and I was walking around looking at things I wanted to get to build a playhouse for my daughter. I saw a 19-year-old in flip flops and khaki shorts with long hair, and he was writing down stuff. I just struck up a conversation with him and asked what he was doing, and he said, 'Well I flip houses.' And I have two college degrees, looking on a third one, and I asked him, 'Did you learn about that in college?' And he said, 'No I didn't go to college.' And I said, 'What about high school?' He said, 'Oh I never really graduated.' And I asked, 'Well are you successful at it?' And he said, 'Yeah, I flip five or six houses a year and I make six figures.' That just really bothered me; I guess I'm driven by pride in a lot of things. But I walked away from that Home

Depot but couldn't get away from the fact that I thought I was smarter than this kid, had more experience this kid, yet he was making more money than I was, and it was all because of real estate.

So, my inspiration was that day, and I went home again, and it just happened that I picked up that book I had with the list of all my goals in it, and the second one on the list was, 'Get involved in real estate.' And I decided that I was going to take action; that 19-year-old kid was my inspiration. I'd like to thank him today; he probably still might be making more money than I am because he started when he was in his late teens, and I didn't really get involved in real estate until I was in my 40s. But he's the one that pushed me because it really bothered me that somebody with a lot less education, but more drive and taking action earlier, would be a successful real estate investor.

That day I went out and made some phone calls and decided I was going to get involved in real estate, and now I'm involved in several facets of it. So that was my inspiration; I found somebody that was doing it, and I just got mad. Maybe that's the wrong way to be inspired, but we're all different and that's what worked for me.

Shannon:
How has your education in real estate changed the way that you invest?

Adam:
When I was 21, I did nothing. I did read; in over 20 years I read over 40 books on real estate, trying to figure out what I wanted to do, but I never took action. What changed it for me and my real estate education is I found a company that had a really good real estate education program with people that I could ask questions to, and I found a community that I could get involved with and other people who were in the same situation that I was and wanted to take action. We grew together so I think the way that real estate education changed the way that I invest is I found the right real estate education that worked for me. It catapulted my drive, my desire, my interest in real estate, and yeah you have to find something that works. I found something that works, a great education.

Shannon:
What is one of the top real estate strategies that you have learned?

Adam:

I think my favorite is creative acquisition strategy. Which is simply the concept that you don't have to just go up to somebody and say, 'You have a house and I'd like to take out a mortgage and buy your house.' Or, 'I'm going to save up all my money until I have enough money to pay cash for a house.' There is a myriad of ways that you can purchase real estate. There are so many options where you can creatively acquire a property, that's the number one strategy that I've found—the sky is the limit. There's just an incredible amount of options out there that I never thought about, would never think about presenting to a seller as an option. But it's not just I'm going to save up and buy, or it's not just I'm going to talk to the bank and borrow money. You can get real estate a whole bunch of different ways.

Shannon:

What are some of those creative ways to acquire a property?

Adam:

Leasing options. Acquiring some property using a lease option where we use the owner's equity in the house and we ask him if he'd be willing to be the bank. We bought a house using a leasing option, it was a $180,000 house. Gave him $20,000 with an option that we would buy the house in two years. So, we bought a $180,000 house for $20,000. He was willing to do it because we were paying him; he was seller financing the house, so we were paying him the money instead of the bank. And he was getting interest, and he essentially sold his house and didn't have to worry about it anymore. We took it over, and in two years after we get the equity in the house we can sell it, still make a profit, and the owner made $20,000 in interest over two years. So, he's happy because he actually got a little bit more than what he wanted out of it. That's a great strategy.

Short sales. Buying foreclosed or pre-foreclosed homes. There's so many different creative ways that you can get a house. But the most important thing in real estate that I have found in all the different ways is it's a win-win for you and a win-win for seller. One of the great things about the education in the community that am investing in is it has to be a win-win for both parties. Unfortunately, there are some real estate investors out in the world who are looking just to take advantage of people and they really don't care . . . the destruction that they leave in their path . . . but I was blessed and fortunate enough to be involved in a community of investors that understand that the deal is not the deal unless everybody wins. That's the kind of real estate investor I want to be; I don't want to take advantage of anybody.

Shannon:
In standard business practices, we're really taught that there is no such thing as a win-win. Somebody always loses. Explain to me how in real estate investing you can have a win-win situation?

Adam:
Well if somebody has a home that they're foreclosed on and they don't see an out. The only option that they see is that they are going to get foreclosed on, because they haven't paid their taxes on their home in a long time or haven't paid their mortgage. If there's an instance where I can basically say, 'I'll be willing to take that over and give you some money, let me buy your house, and I gave you $10,000, and I can get you caught up on your mortgage and I'll pay your back taxes.' They get the benefit. Number one, they get some money to start off. Number two, they don't have to go through the foreclosure process, have their credit affected. I get a better deal on the house, and we both walk away with some money. A lot of times people that are in foreclosure are looking for an out, but the banks really only have one option: give us the money or we're going to take these steps.

Now the people who sell the house are aware of that initially but sometimes people get in over their heads, or circumstances in their lives change and they are just looking for a way out, so they can start over, or have the water that they're essentially drowning in go down, so they can keep their head above it. Creatively if you can give somebody that option, where they can get some money to get back on their feet, and they can get out of the load of the house that's bearing down on them, then I consider that a total win-win, and everybody comes out ahead.

I would challenge those who say that there's no such thing as a win-win; I've been involved in a lot of impossible situations that would challenge that belief. I've never had a deal where I've walked away, and somebody didn't say, 'Hey that was a good thing for me I made money at the end of it.' I mean, I've never not had that deal— people are always grateful for the opportunity that they had to get out of the mess.

Shannon:

If someone was going to start in real estate, what would you recommend they do first?

Adam:

Well everybody's a little bit different. What worked for me after 20 years of checking out real estate books from the library, or buying them online, or buying them at Barnes and Nobles, what worked for me was getting involved in a good education. Getting a mentor, somebody that has already done what you're doing and just shadowing them, asking them questions; you have to find the right person. Sometimes you might even have to pay some money to get involved in what other people are doing because anything that works well in life to help you to move ahead is going to come at some kind of a cost. So, for me I had to put some skin in the game and put my money where my mouth was and get involved with a mentor, get involved with a team, and take action.

Shannon:

How has mentors in your real estate investing helped you to navigate potential pitfalls?

Adam:

Well I have a really interesting story about that. When I first got with my person that mentored me, I was looking at a wholesale deal which meant that somebody else found a house, they didn't want to put the work into it, they bought it for a really, really, really good price, and they were willing to sell it to me for $20,000, which allowed some room for me to make some money. I was really excited about that because there was a fair amount of money in my opinion that could be made on this house. I asked my mentor to come take a look at it with me, and he was really excited, and the next day he was willing to sign on the deal. I hadn't done too many thorough inspections on the house and so I asked him to look at it with me.

He walked around, and this was an old house that had dog crap all over the place. The previous owner had let their dogs live in the house for three months, and dishes were piled up all over the place, and you couldn't walk 18 inches without stepping in some kind of mess. I could look past all that and see the potential of the house, and my mentor walked with me downstairs after a little while and he said,

'What do you think?' And I said, 'This looks like a deal to me.' And he said, 'Well I noticed something; let's go look in the back.' The previous owner had added on to the house by framing some walls and not putting in a concrete foundation. He said, 'What about this?'

He pointed it out to me and I just hadn't seen it, I just had kind of glanced over it and hadn't made a mental connection there. And he talked to me about and told me if I was going to sell the house, it would be inspected, and I couldn't just dig under that the way that this is built and put a foundation in. And he walked through that with me and showed me in the end that the house wasn't going to make any money because of the work I had to put into it.

So, in that instance he saved me from a huge potential pitfall. He had the knowledge, I didn't. He was patient and walked me through the process, asked me some questions. It was obvious he was trying to see where I was at and help me see some of the things that just weren't obvious to me, that were obvious to him. He saved me a lot of money in that first deal. I didn't get involved in it, and I'm grateful for it because I know a lot more now about what to look for or what to keep my eyes open for.

Shannon:
In your business how do you help other people learn more about real estate?

Adam:
I found that I have a passion for taking anybody who wants to be where I was several years ago, or they're ready to take the next step and are ready to take action but are looking for direction. I have a lot of passion for saying, 'Hey this is what worked for me, what works for you?' One of the interesting things about real estate is that there's a host of different potential ways that you can make money, and I don't invest in all of them, I specialize in a couple of them, and I know about the other ones and I dabble in them; I'll probably get involved in them. I get a lot of personal satisfaction in finding out what drives other people, what interests them, what motivates them in a particular aspect of real estate, and watching them get excited and having success.

There is a lot of fun in watching somebody get their first deal and go through it. I understand what it's like to step into some of the pitfalls, I understand what it's like to take that first scary step. Now that I've done it and I've found success, I'm able to encourage other people to do the same thing to help better their lives. There's just a tremendous amount of satisfaction you get by watching somebody else achieve success in something that they want to get better at.

Shannon:

What advice would you give to someone who is allowing fear to hold them back from starting their real estate investing career?

Adam:

Well I guess I'd say two things. I'm a big quote guy, I have a book of quotes and every time I find something that is positive and motivating I write it down, and several of them I have memorized. Dale Carnegie is attributed to have said, 'If you want to conquer fear do not sit at home and just think about it. Go out and get busy.' So, the first thing that I would say is if you want to conquer your fear you need to address it, instead of just hiding behind a wall. Go out and get busy and find ways to get past that. The second thing is I've just finished reading The Success Principles by Jack Canfield and one of the main principles in that book is that you have control over three things in your life: what you think, the images that you visualize, and the actions you take.

So, if you want to conquer your fear you have to identify what it is that scares you, and then decide that you're going to take action and overcome that. If you don't, you will never, ever, get past that fear. You have to choose that you're going to overcome it. So that would be my advice to people, ask them 'What is it that scares you about this?' And then see if they want to make a decision and say, 'Do you want to take this straight on and conquer it? If you do, let's go out and get busy and take action.'

Shannon:

What is the number one mistake an individual makes when buying their first investment property?

Adam:

Not being thorough. Real estate is a pretty fast-moving business; properties don't last too long on the market. One of the dangers is you must make an offer on a property and be quick, otherwise someone who knows more than you do is going to do that. I have found that if you make an offer on a property one of the biggest mistakes you can do is not give yourself 10 to 14 days in your offer to thoroughly analyze the house, not understanding that you do have some time there to get out of it if you want.

Nobody is the best at everything, so it's important that you can get you're your mentor, or other people you trust, and have them walk the properties to see if they have any red flags that you might not see. There's that old proverb that says, 'Four eyes are better than two, and six eyes are better than four.' So, use your friends in your community; use your team to help you make a good decision. Don't just think that you're going to do it all yourself because if you do that sometimes you're going to end up getting in trouble.

Shannon:
When you began your real estate investing career, how important was it for you to establish a team to help you be successful?

Adam:
It was incredibly important, and I'm still looking to add the right people to my team. All the time I zone into people and find out that their strengths are better than my strengths. There's that popular moniker that notes that 'team' stands for 'Together everyone achieves more.' And I understood that earlier on. I may believe I have strength, but if I go to the gym and I can bench press 285 and I see somebody who can bench press 385, he's obviously put more work in or has better techniques than I do. So as long as I'm not too prideful, I can go up to him and say, 'Hey, what are you doing?' And he's successful, so he's willing to say 'This is what I'm doing. This how I eat clean, this is how I work out, this is how I maximize my rest.'

You know, in any concept of a team you can't be so arrogant that you think you're the best at everything. You need to surround yourself with people that you recognize and accept are smarter than you and really get their knowledge. Ask them to teach you, and be humble enough to learn from them. Be willing to realize that you can make more money if you are willing to accept that they're better than you in a couple of things, and ask for their advice and be willing to pay them when they give it to you in certain instances. 'Together everyone achieves more' is an absolute real concept; you just have to be willing to recognize, again, that other people are smarter than you in a lot of things.

Shannon:

How do you feel that learning multiple investing strategies protects and accelerates your investing success?

Adam:

Well on a smaller scale I think it's the same concept as the stock market. I don't invest in just one stock, with some of the investments I have I diversify because, number one, it's good to have multiple options, and number two, different things go up and down in real estate. Whether you're investing in commercial real estate or you're flipping houses or you're looking for short sale opportunities, you need to diversify because there's always little hot pockets in the market. You want to generate as many income streams as you can because something might be hotter than something else in the market in six months.

I have a 401(k) that I use to help me invest, but you can be an aggressive investor, or you can be a moderate investor in a 401(k), and you'll invest in different properties because some will go up faster than others, some are more aggressive than others, and it's the same concept for real estate. It's stupid to put all your eggs in one basket because if that basket or if that particular investment strategy that you're using has a problem because of something that happened in the market you're going to lose—you have to diversify.

Shannon:

You know, you said earlier that homes don't stay on the market very long and that they move quickly. So, is real estate investing success dependent on a strong economy?

Adam:

Oh, I would say absolutely not. Right now, the market's hot. Right after 2008 a lot of people lost a lot of money, in my opinion because, as we've discussed before, maybe they had too many eggs in one basket, or they got a little bit too greedy. But I know dozens, if not more, of successful investors that made a lot of money because when properties depreciated, and people got in over their head and were looking for a way out, there were several investors that said, 'Look, I'm willing to offer you this, and pay you some money to get out of that situation.' And they were able to buy properties at lower values, and then over time they just waited because the real estate market over time is always a very profitable venture. Properties always go up in value, and so they were able to buy a lot of properties at lower values and just watch them over the next few years gain back their equity.

There was an investor about 30 miles away who was looking to sell several apartment complexes that he bought in 2008/9, after the market fell, because he got them for good deals. Now he has an incredible amount of assets, and he's made his money, now he's looking at retiring and move on and just have fun in a different way. So, I don't believe in any way, shape, or form that you can only make money in the real estate when the market's good. You need to be able to diversify your way of thinking. If the markets down there's a way to make money; if the markets up, then there're ways to make money.

Shannon:
Tell me one way that you can make money when the market is down?

Adam:
You can buy properties that people have gotten over their heads in. The banks getting ready to foreclose, the banks want to get as much money as they can, which is often not going to be as much as they loaned on it. Like we discussed before, if somebody is in over their head and are looking for a way out, the banks haven't offered them that way out, and you can go in and offer them money to start off on and buy that property. You can offer to catch up their payments, so they don't have to go through foreclosure and lose all their credit.

I've been talking to a friend about buying some of his multi-family properties; that's how he ended up getting over 40 properties—he wasn't cut throat about it. Whenever I get into a business deal with somebody, I need to get a feel for what kind of investor they are because if somebody is willing to take advantage of somebody in a really bad situation, then I don't really want to do business with that person. But if they were able to help people and end up having a positive relationship, then I would like to do business with those guys because I believe in if you treat people bad that's coming back to bite you in the end.

Shannon:
What's one way that you can invest in real estate when the market is up?

Adam:

Right now, the market is pretty hot, and there's a lot of distressed properties out there that need some improvement. In my area in Idaho, there are houses between $130,000 and $190,000 that are distressed and it is really hot. People want to buy in that price range. So, in this area, when we find a distressed property that needs a lot of work, if we can get it for a good deal, we'll put the money into it to turn it back into a nice property that is up to date, and we can sell it and make a bit of money—that's one great way. We've flipped several houses that we were able to get for a deal because for whatever reason people left them, they foreclosed on them. If we find a property and we can make money on it, then that's it. In Idaho, that's a great price range for us to be able to be profitable at.

Shannon:

How does real estate allow you to earn masses and passive income?

Adam:

Well that's a good question. Somebody who's just getting started out in real estate obviously would like to do something like flipping houses because they want to make money fast, and get massive income; you can do that all day long in real estate if you keep your eyes open. Passive income, I think for most people is a harder thing because it's a harder thought process to invest in a property that is only going to give you a few hundred dollars over time every month.

I have a few rental properties. We have some renters in there that are paying $1500 a month. We give them a little discount if they pay on time, which is great incentive as they've never missed a payment and they've never been late on a payment. So, their payments pay higher than rent and there's a little bit extra even I pay insurance to get that passive income. If I can go out and flip 5, or 6, or 8, or 10 houses in year, and I can go out and find one that I think could be a really good rental opportunity. The money's right, the price is right, it's in a good location, and I can rent it pretty easy over long term, get some consistent money out of it.

If I can just buy one of those properties and do one every year, after 10 years I will have 10 rental properties. If I can get $300 or $400 a month in rent over expenses, that becomes $4800 over 12 months. If I can do that year after year, I'll have $50,000 of income coming in from rental properties. You can build a sizable passive income portfolio, and you don't have to do it really aggressively. It's a really smart way to invest for the long term. The biggest problems that people have are they are too scared and they don't think they can do it, and number two they think they can buy these properties if they save up enough money, or if they willing to put up their own house so that they can get another mortgage, and there are just so many different ways that you can be profitable in real estate, and make money, if you have the right education on how to go about it.

Shannon:
What is cash flow, and why should it be such an important focus of your business?

Adam:
Cash flow is the amount of money that flows in and out of your business. It's obviously turbulent for your business because you want to make sure you have as much coming in as you have going out.

Shannon:
Why do you think people fail at real estate?

Adam:
There are probably a couple of reasons. Number one, they get involved in real estate by jumping in; they say, 'I have some money I'm going to buy a house,' and they just don't know what they're doing. You don't make money on a house by fixing it up and selling it, you make money on a house in your offer. It needs to be structured correctly, contractually it needs to have things set up, so all the bases are covered.

People will just get into a house thinking they know some rough numbers thinking It makes sense to them, but they don't have all the answers. They might just do 3 out of 10, and one major mistake in real estate can really set you back if you don't do things correctly. So, I would say the biggest reason that people fail is because they don't know what they're doing. They think they know what they're doing. But they don't know what they're doing.

Shannon:
If someone wanted to invest in multi-family dwellings, what do they need to know?

Adam:

That it's a bigger investment generally than just residential housing. You are dependent on multiple families when you set things up contractually. When you buy the house, you have to understand vacancy rates and your total amount of income streams from buying a multi-family unit. The reality is you're not going to have somebody in there all the time. You have to do the math right and understand that there's going to be some increased costs.

I think if somebody's going to get involved in multi-family units, it's a great investment, but again you have to know what you're getting into. You have to know that you're doing the math right, you have to know that you're setting up the deal right. You have to understand that there's probably going to be some higher maintenance costs involved, and you just have to understand the deal before you get into it.

Shannon:

Though obviously your goal in a multi-family dwelling would be 100 percent occupancy. But what's the realistic goal?

Adam:

I think it depends on the area. In Idaho where I live they're building a number of apartment complexes because there just aren't enough rentals. The market does have a lot of impact on rentals, and when its really hot people want to buy houses, and when the market's down they want to rent and be a little safer. The world is made up of a lot of different people, and there are always going to be people that want to rent houses. Ideally, I would say that if you were in for 70 to 80 percent of the time, then that would be realistic goal to work to math around.

From my experience you're going to have some renters that are going to rent your properties for a decade, or longer. They're going to be fantastic tenants that never miss a payment, that always pay on time, and don't mess up your building because they take good care of it and treat it like their own. But there are units that people destroy just because that's the way they live; it's not theirs so they don't take any ownership in it, and you're going to have to put some extra money into constantly fixing up those things. That's a part of being a landlord; in a multi-family unit you have to maximize and set yourself up to find the best tenants, but you are always going to have challenges. You're never going to have a situation where every tenant is perfect, that's just never going to happen.

Shannon:
Most millionaires and billionaires have investments in commercial real estate. Why do you think that is?

Adam:
I think several reasons. Commercial real estate has great appreciation values. A lot of the assets that you can rent out or lease are assets secured by leases, and so that presents a little bit more stability. Another great option is you place debt on the commercial asset, often which is several times the value of the equity. So, you can get more money out of it and use it for greater leverage. There are also many tax benefits, the mortgage interest and appreciation deductions offset a lot of the income you have as an owner of that property. So, there are several great investment opportunities in real estate that give you some great advantages.

Shannon:
Last question, what type of legacy do you want to leave?

Adam:
Obviously I want to be successful personally. But my personal success is just going to be one step; my long-term goal is after I achieve success in real estate, I would like to be somebody that passes it around—I'd like to be a mentor, I'd like to be an instructor. I believe that in my community all the instructors are people who have achieved success in the past. They know what they're doing, they get a lot of personal satisfaction out of it, and after that they realize that they just find a lot of joy in helping others achieve that same satisfaction in growing. That's the legacy I would like to leave. I love what I do—I really enjoy helping other people succeed. Probably as important as being a real estate investor, I would just like to see somebody in the store or somewhere that I did a deal with, and they will come up and shake my hand and say hello without any harsh feelings.

The most important thing about my legacy is I always want to be honest in everything that I'm doing with everybody and make sure I treat them fairly. If I do that I'll always have a community of friends and when people walk past my grave some would comment, 'You know what? He was a good guy, and he treated people fair, and he helped me achieve success.' So, I don't think I'm anything more special than anybody else, I just want to be a good person, and I don't need to have my face on a mountain. I just want people to think good of me as the real estate investor who was a good person.

Brian Visconti

Brian Visconti grew up in western Pennsylvania studying mathematics with multiple minors at Saint Vincent College in Latrobe, Pennsylvania. Brian began his professional career as a high school teacher before transitioning into a position as a fundraiser for volunteer fire departments and ambulance services in the Midwest. He simultaneously began to own and operate multiple retail seasonal concepts in Indiana and Illinois. He then transferred those skills into owning his own merchandising company servicing well-known companies from coast to coast. During his early adventures, he began to purchase investment rental properties, and he currently owns multiple single-family homes. He continues to expand his portfolio one house at a time since purchasing his first property in 1998.

Too excited about life to retire, he intends to provide quality housing for low- to moderate-income families for years to come. As a former teacher, he is always looking for ways to help others improve their lives physically, mentally, spiritually, and financially.

Shannon:
According to Forbes magazine, real estate is one of the top three ways people become wealthy. As a real estate expert, why do you feel this is the case?

Brian:
I do know that my uncle was the first in my family to use real estate as a wealth creation tool. If it wasn't for him, I probably wouldn't even be in real estate. He's probably the wealthiest relative that I have. I just know that when I was 12 years old, he came and visited. He had plenty of time to travel. Not being that old of a gentleman, I figured that he was doing something better than my dad. So I, through the process of my life, entertained the idea of buying real estate. I learned as much as I could about real estate knowing that's the vehicle that most wealthy people use to become successful.

Shannon:
If someone was going to start in real estate investing, what would you recommend they do first?

Brian:
The first thing is I would get an education and/or a mentor, someone's that's already successful in the business, and learn from their experience. Learn things not to do in real estate so that you can avoid pitfalls and simple mistakes that would cost potentially thousands of dollars.

Shannon:
How have mentors in your real estate investing helped you to navigate potential pitfalls?

Brian:
I don't know if I should mention specific people, but I started out in the business because of a good friend of mine, Chris Albin. Basically, he was successful in real estate, and I utilized his expertise and knowledge in order to learn a base system that would allow me to become successful.

Shannon:

When you began your real estate investing career, how important was it for you to establish a team to help you be successful?

Brian:

First thing I had to accomplish was finding a method to buy property. Once you acquire the first property it's a matter of learning the who and how to fix it. You realize it's not the most efficient use of your time hanging drywall and painting for example. So the goal was to find other people who could actually work on the house. And then it became a team of professionals, a lawyer, and eventually an accountant to solve the inevitable day-to-day problems that come with a business.

Shannon:

In your business how do you help other people learn more about real estate?

Brian:

I always try to educate people about the process of buying, selling, or renting real estate. If they want to learn information from me, I'm certainly open to sharing information. I'm a big believer of buying into an education system or mentoring program that will help teach the business. I know couldn't have made it by myself. I know how difficult it is for other people, especially if they've never invested before, to take that first step.

Shannon:

What is cash flow and why should it be such an important focus of your business?

Brian:

Well, cash flow is like the difference blood makes to the body. Without cash flow, the business would not survive. A business can't survive without money coming in, even to maintain a basic baseline. If you don't have cash flow, bills would not get paid. Cash flow pays the mortgage, insurance, water bills, power bills, and taxes, not to mention paying for laborers and professional to repair and maintain the building. All businesses would have to have cash flow. It wouldn't survive if they didn't make deposits.

Shannon:

How does real estate allow you to earn massive and passive income?

Brian:

You can utilize the real estate in two facets. The first would be through either fixing a property to flip it or to buy and hold. Either way, the key in real estate is to buy low. Whether you want to fix and flip or buy and hold, if you didn't buy the property correctly at the right price you can't make any money.

So, whether you use the real estate for passive income over an extended period of time or to make one time capital gains, you will need a cash stream that actually allows the tenant or the client to pay down the mortgage. While you simply acquire use of the property, rental income pays down the mortgage, hopefully gaining active appreciation on the building.

Shannon:

Do you feel that real estate investing success is dependent on a strong economy?

Brian:

Well, I started investing myself back in 2000. And so I went through several ups and downs. I saw a very difficult time in 2007 during the banking crisis. It was very difficult to acquire money to even survive. Credit card companies slashed available credit. It was a rough period. I had a couple houses that had some tenant challenges. It took a little bit of effort to get through those times. But typically, in a high market, you can acquire a property at a lower price and/or a lower interest rate, which is always a good thing. You just need to know where to look and what approach to take. No matter what the economy throws at us, there are always individuals that have problems whether that's job loss, foreclosure, divorce, moving because of a job transfer, or even death. There's always some kind of challenge that people face just because of life. It's never really difficult to find properties. It's just a matter of whether someone is willing to work to find those properties.

Shannon:

You said you've been investing since 2000. So over the last 18 years, how has your education changed the way that you invest?

Brian:

Back in 2000, I did invest in different educational programs. If somebody was advertising to me, I'd invest in their program. My greatest aid probably was my mentor. Whenever he would recommend a real estate course that he attended, then I would go take it.

The first thing that I learned was about probate. I actually went to a formal class and spent a couple of days learning how to acquire properties utilizing probate. That led to other facets that he now teaches. That has certainly helped me acquire properties. Now my mentor has not needed to help me find a property since I took the class.

Shannon:

How can a real estate investor benefit from notes, tax liens, and deeds?

Brian:

Everybody's situation is different. Buying property—or at least property through tax liens, deeds, and mortgages—is just another avenue to invest in. If somebody doesn't have hands on experience with property, it's pretty easy to just acquire one as a mortgagee or as a tax lien holder to control a property. You know you can get a higher interest rate than the bank is offering. You can negotiate pretty good terms depending upon what county you're in with a tax lien.

You can also acquire notes where you lock in interest rates that would do much better than a bank note. I know that the banks pay like a .25 percent as a CD. As a mortgagee, you can kind of pick the investment vehicle you want to invest in and earn 6 percent or 12 percent. Those vehicles are out there. You just have to look for them or find the information to learn where to find them.

Shannon:

How can an individual benefit from a lease option?

Brian:

If you don't necessarily want the property you can acquire access to the property through a lease option. If you have not decided if you actually want the property, a lease option is great. You can wait for the property value to appreciate on the property before taking outright ownership. That's great for a decision at the end of an option.

You could then sell the option to another buyer. It basically allows for a timeframe to make a decision on the property.

Shannon:
When you're doing a fix and flip, what do you want to look out for?

Brian:
In my market, I really don't do fix and flips. My valuation has been stagnant. By the time you put your money into it, it's just better to hold onto it and let a tenant pay down a property. But the key would be the investment—you would have to run the numbers and make sure it would make sense.

Most people can never judge how long it's going to take to repair the building. So they either get caught because they didn't plan for enough time, didn't think of all the actual expenses that would occur, or they don't plan an exit strategy. That's the most difficult thing with the fix and flip.

Shannon:
When you're looking for a buy and hold, a property to acquire and put in your portfolio, what's one of the things that you're looking for?

Brian:
The basic model that I follow is the numbers. I want to acquire a property at the lowest price possible that's a fair value for the person that I'm buying the property from. That number has to justify whatever rent I would get and the fix up costs. Buying a property in Danville is a little different than most markets. If I buy a property for $15,000, and I want to put $5,000 into it, I need to have a rent that justifies that.

If you're in a market that you can buy a property for $100,000 then you need to make sure you can justify that with your fix up cost. It's all about math.

Shannon:
If somebody wanted to invest in multi-family dwellings, do they need to do anything different, or what do they need to know?

Brian:

The challenge with multi-family units and the reason I like single-family homes is because the tenant typically is my customer and the neighbor is not my customer. In a multi-family the neighbor is also my customer. So whenever they complain about their neighbor they're also complaining about my tenant.

It becomes a little challenging. And if, for example, you run into a tenant that has a bug problem in a multi-family unit, everybody's now got the same bug problem. Then it becomes my problem. In multi-family units the bug problem can be traced back to one tenant. Once your building gets bugs, you as the owner own the challenge.

Shannon:

What advice would you give to someone that was allowing fear to hold them back from starting their real estate investing?

Brian:

Fear is, from my perspective, based upon a lack of information. If you're afraid of something you just don't have enough correct information to justify making an informed decision. You could correct that through the right friends or a good education program. You must find someone or something that you can count on for good advice.

Everybody's got the same problems in life. Don't reinvent the wheel. Someone has already solved your problem; your task is to find that right person to answer your question.

Shannon:

How has real estate changed your life?

Brian:

It has given me freedom. I know my high school reunion is coming up, actually this weekend, and it'll be interesting to know everybody has jobs they go to. I'm already to the point where I don't have to work. I won't tell them that, but it's a nice place to be in. I can go on vacation, do things I want to do when I want to do them. I still have things that I do that require my time, but I do most of the work that I do because I enjoy it. It's not because I have to do it. So I look at my life as if I don't work a day. I have a lot of fun and get to see a lot of people. Been to almost all 50 states. I'm only missing Idaho at this point and Hawaii and Alaska, and I should have all that accomplished by the end of this year. It's just pretty fun.

Shannon:

If you're starting with little money or poor credit, what are some strategies to get into real estate?

Brian:

I kind of started with no money. I found a couple people that had money that I could utilize. Either they had a property that I could simply take over the payments, or I found a mentor that wanted to help me invest. That's typically been my strategy.

The older you get the more you're going to learn this. Most people don't put their own money into a deal. They use other people's money. It's just safer that way. Whether you have no money/credit or you do, most people don't want to use their own money, whether that is a credit card, or an investor, or an investor with a property they can't do anything with, for example, they're moving or something. You can actually just take over the payments, manage the property, and rent it out.

Shannon:

Now, how do you find the people with the homes?

Brian:

There are strategies, utilizing the education, to find and acquire people. A great resource is your local courthouse. Find property owners that are having trouble with tenants and talk to them. Another way is for landlords to join a local organization. There are a lot of landlords that are wanting to retire because of health and age issues. The property has already done for them what they needed it to do. If you join a real estate group, or look in the newspaper, there are landlords selling property at an affordable price.

They're not that difficult to find if you know where to look.

Shannon:

How do you minimize the risk of investing so that you can maximize your success?

Brian:

The key to real estate, it doesn't matter what market you're in, is always to be able to buy a property at or below market value. If the property has a distressed situation, the seller needs to discount the property to get rid of it. You can convince somebody that it's in their best interest to do so. It's easier to take over payments before the mortgage gets way behind. I will rent the building and it will pay the mortgage. You know, say they move now and have got two house payments. Their job only pays for one, that's really not a good situation.

And if they're out of state, it's not a good situation. What I can do for someone in that situation is to help them out. I tell them that I have a solution to their problem. This is what the numbers look like. Though they think it's worth $100,000, they owe only $80,000. So I can give the $80,000 owed. That number is actually invested in solving the problem so they don't have to deal with the tax bill, mortgage payments, electric, sewer, etc. I can do that all for them. And I'm local. I can solve their problem.

Shannon:

Most millionaires and billionaires have investments in commercial real estate. Why is that?

Brian:

The reason wealthy people would acquire real estate on a commercial level is simply the numbers. I deal with small residential properties because that's where numbers look best for me. But the bigger your number, that is, the bigger your bank account, the bigger the number has to be to justify putting your money.

You don't want to make a lot of little deals when you have plenty of money in the bank to do a big deal. Typically, depending on how you acquire property and how you develop property, all can lead to wealth creation. That's where wealth is.

Shannon:

What type of legacy do you want to leave?

Brian:

My goal has always been to help as many people as I can. Maybe that's helping individuals get out of a problem property for them. The people that work for me, it gives them a job, a career, a life that they normally wouldn't have had. I know that every decision I make affects other people's lives. Everyone's decisions are like that, whether or not we look at it that way. I consciously chose to set it up that way. I know I'm fine whatever I do. But I make some decisions based on how I affect other people.

I wouldn't be where I am without people helping me. My goal in life is to help give a hand and pick people up from where they are. I want people to say, 'He did his best to help whenever he could.'

Joshua White

Joshua White is an accomplished entrepreneur, Real estate investor, published author, and motorsport professional. Joshua is the CEO and founder of R3 ENTERPRISES LLC and Projects Motorsport.

Joshua's hobbies include pro racing, travel, and creating memories with family and friends. He is a distinguished father of one 15-year old daughter, Madelynn Grace White. Armed with education and minimal mentorship, Joshua has managed to bust through the expectations of society and become a great success in real estate investing, pro motorsports, and leadership, while helping others do the same. Relationships and family are the main foundations of Joshua's approach to life. He is pioneering the path to retiring inside of his business and creating a long-lasting legacy for his family and friends.

CEO - Projects Motorsport/ R3 Enterprises

Shannon:

*As a real estate expert, why do you feel that, according to Forbes maga-
zine, real estate is one of the top three ways people become wealthy?*

Joshua:

A lot of it has to do with owning a small business and creating a business, with the tax strategies. This country was built on real estate,
and I believe that the knowledge of real estate, and owning and running a real estate business, is what actually keeps this country moving.

Shannon:

Yes, it is. What inspired you to get into real estate?

Joshua:

I was in quite a dark place with a new baby on the way. I was working
in professional motor sports. I owned it, and I worked for many
wealthy people. One of the reasons I got into real estate was mainly
because the people I was around were wealthy, and I wasn't. And I
continually asked them all about how they became that way, and what
businesses to run, and they all had one thing in common: real estate—owning it and leveraging it.

Shannon:

*If someone was wanting to get started in real estate, what would you
recommend they do first?*

Joshua:

Seek, find, and invest in the proper up-to-date knowledge. There are
a number of platforms out there to teach you just enough to get yourself and your investors in trouble and lose money. Seek the strategies
that you will carry all the way through to the end. Real estate takes
time. It will not happen overnight, and you cannot expect a so-called
home run every time. Real estate is a craft like anything else. True
wealth needs to be crafted to live, carry on, and NEVER die.

So what I did is I scoured about for quite a while. I spent x amount
of dollars seeking the education but ended up at a roadblock every
time. Until late 2013. I absolutely stumbled onto the standard of what
education could be. It was more than real estate. They taught you the
organic stuff, like credit management, building entities, taxes and legal

matters, choosing your proper investor ID. I researched it and Invested in myself. It required massive action and, most of all, the personal development that was created. This was priceless!!

Shannon:
How has your education in real estate changed the way that you invest?

Joshua:
It has taught me how to work inside of the strategies that make creating true wealth possible. It is much more than fix and flips and buying and listing homes. I now see that I can retire inside of my business instead of from it. There are ways to build legacies that last forever. And that is what I am after.

My first option would be to be a buy and hold investor, which holds the property and creates passive cash flow. Education has also changed the way I look at land, and my strategies for rentals. The new Airbnb market is becoming quite the cash flow creator with many more options than long-term rentals. There are so many different ways to create cash flow and create win-win solutions which in return create relationships, which is the true currency that brings it all together.

Shannon:
Why do you think that people fail at real estate?

Joshua:
Because they make the money the focus, and they're not educated. Like I said earlier, there are many different strategies to real estate, and one property can look like one strategy but have five different exit strategies possible. Without proper knowledge, they don't know that, and they get into transactions that are over leveraged, and they end up losing their money and end up hurting their lives.

Shannon:
Explain to me a little bit more about your buy and hold strategy. How does real estate allow you to earn massive and passive income?

Joshua:
Well the massive would come from buying an investment property, fixing it up, rehabbing it, and then selling it. Wholesaling is another.

The buy and hold strategy is a great way to create long-term wealth. The buy and hold is how you build your portfolio and create massive leverage in this country. The more rentals and more property you own, the more options you have with other investments, and the cash flow is plentiful.

Shannon:
What is cash flow, and why should it be such an important focus of your business?

Joshua:
Cash flow is basically the profit after the bills are paid. And it is what fuels the rest of your business to keep it moving fluidly.

Shannon:
When doing a fix and flip, what do you want to look out for?

Joshua:
Well—everything. You want to look at the qualifying problems first, which are the things that the inspector's going to look at. When the homeowner comes and needs to get a loan on a property, you need to have the qualifying upgrades done, or you will probably have a challenge selling the property. So it's basically the big qualifying upgrades that are the biggest part of a flip. All the rest is excess.

Shannon:
If someone wanted to invest in multifamily dwellings, what do they need to know that is different?

Joshua:
Add two zeroes onto everything. That is my next goal. Education is vital to multifamily.

Shannon:
How can an individual benefit from a lease option?

Joshua:
A lease option is great for the buyer and the seller. If you get a home that somebody wants to purchase, but can't get clearance on because of their credit or a financial challenge, you can lease it to them for a

period of time until they fix their credit or other issue arises. The seller actually creates cash flow and the person leasing gets the time to fix their problem. It's a win-win situation for all parties.

Shannon:
When doing a short sale, what should you anticipate?

Joshua:
Well the name, first of all, is wrong. It should be anticipated as a long purchase, not a short sale. And you should think at least nine months on a short sale. The biggest thing on a short sale is you're going to negotiate with the bank. So you either need to have a team member that is good with that, or you need to become good at that, and the way to become good at it is with knowledge and education.

The biggest problem with short sales is people go into them without negotiating skills, and it is a 9-month to 12-month negotiation. Now not every deal goes that way. I've seen a short sale go in four months. So you at least need to anticipate at 9 to 12 months, and if you're paying costs, this really matters.

Shannon:
Most millionaires and billionaires have investments in commercial real estate. Why do you think that is?

Joshua:
Because business is always growing, and it's never going to falter. That's an entire different facet of real estate. Commercial is a whole different way of looking at things. Commercial real estate is like what I said for multi-families: you take the number of what a regular property would be and you add a couple zeroes to the math. Commercial has a good amount of law knowledge in it as well. The investing is different from a single-family home and the biggest part of success how serious you take your education.

Shannon:
Do you feel that real estate investing success is dependent on a strong economy?

Joshua:

No, not at all. A creative investor or an educated individual can make money in any market. A down market is actually where the wealth swap happens. Because when you buy a property, you make most of your money on the purchase, not on the sale.

Shannon:

Explain this to me a little bit further. If you're spending money on a property, how are you making money on the purchase and not the sale?

Joshua:

Because it's how you buy the property that makes the money, not how you sell it. So your knowledge of your strategy coming in is how you create your profit. You will need to have the numbers right in the beginning to make the end work.

Shannon:

When you began your real estate investing career, how important was it for you to establish a team to help you be successful?

Joshua:

A team is vital. Because as human beings, we have special things we can do and we have things we don't do. A lot of people think that they can keep everything in-house and do everything themselves. But the importance of building a team is that you build people and relationships that specialize in certain areas. Everyone executes their knowledge and specialty and it makes the transactions much more efficient.

Shannon:

How have mentors in your real estate investing helped you to navigate potential pitfalls?

Joshua:

Having mentors is like getting a second opinion at the doctor. As an investor, you get into the numbers and you might experience a little tunnel vision sometimes. A good investor will often ask somebody on their team to look at a deal and offer a second set of eyes. I have asked mentors to do that for me and it has saved my bootie.

Shannon:

In your business, how do you help other people learn more about real estate?

Joshua:

I help them understand the aspects of correct knowledge. That's the same thing that my mentor did for me, and now I cannot get enough of it!

Shannon:

What advice would you give to someone who is allowing fear to hold them back from starting their real estate investing career?

Joshua:

Fear is a lack of knowledge, which creates lack of confidence. For instance, when somebody goes to a new job their first day, they're worried about how they look and what people think about them. If you talk to the same person 60 days later, they don't really stress about how they are dressed. They don't worry because they have created confidence through the knowledge and training that they have received through the time they have had the job. Knowledge breeds confidence. Confidence breeds action.

Shannon:

What is velocity banking?

Joshua:

Velocity banking is the art of using credit as leverage and cash as velocity. It's a successful strategy that takes knowledge and responsibility. Basically, you learn to leverage the bank's money at 0 percent, instead of asking for money on an amortized schedule. You are making money leveraging the bank's money. I have worked for a few years to be able to get these credit lines. I started as an investor with a 460 credit score. I now have a 782, and it's because of my credit repair and my credit management knowledge. One you learn velocity banking, your investing can reach much higher levels of ownership, leverage, and both personal and business credit, which is vital to long term wealth creation.

Shannon:

What type of legacy do you want to leave?

Joshua:

I want to leave a legacy of honesty and integrity. I will help build 12-15 millionaires. One of my goals is for them to be able to sit on any beach and be able to say, "Josh was right, and we are blessed that we listened to him". That's the legacy I want to leave.

Woody Woodward

Woody Woodward dropped out of high school at age 16, was a millionaire by 26 and flat broke by age 27. After clawing his way out of financial ruin he built four different multi-million dollar companies before he turned 40. Through overcoming this adversity Mr. Woodward has become a bestselling author of fifteen books about turning tragedy into triumph. Having interviewed over 2,500 people around the world for his research, he is the pioneer and founder of Your Emotional Fingerprint™. Understanding this cutting edge human technology allows one to strip back the layers of excuses and build a proper foundation for mass achievement in one's personal life, relationships and career. Emotional Fingerprint was chosen as one of the leading techniques to be presented to the United Nations to assist them in reaching their millennial goals.

His latest project is inspiring entrepreneurs with M.O.N.E.Y. Matrix™ daily videos that help them reach their goals, make more money and find fulfillment in their careers. He has shared his cutting edge techniques on ABC, CBS, NBC, FOX and Forbes.

Contact Info:
www.GetMoneyMatrix.com
www.MeetWoody.com

Shannon:

According to Forbes Magazine, real estate is one of the top three ways that people become wealthy. As a real estate expert, why do you feel that this is the case?

Woody:

Real estate is the only investment I know of where you have a tangible, physical product that, even if the market goes down, you can still use. Yes, you can say stocks are tangible, but in reality they're not. Yes, you can lease them out, you can do calls and you can do puts on them, but with real estate, even if the market crashes, you can physically rent that property. You get a tax write-off if you are renting the property; so to me, real estate has always been, looking back in history, one of the top ways to generate revenue.

Shannon:

Do you have an opinion on whether commercial real estate or residential real estate is a better investment?

Woody:

I have friends who do both. I personally have always done residential. As for my friends who do commercial real estate it adds a zero to their net worth. If you're going to make a hundred thousand dollars on flipping a residential property, you'll make about a million flipping a commercial property; so it's the same game, just bigger numbers. If you have the resources to do it, most billionaires do it in commercial property, not residential. A lot of millionaires do residential property.

Shannon:

How hard is it to get started in residential real estate if you don't have a lot of money?

Woody:

That's the great thing about residential versus commercial; it doesn't take hardly anything with residential. Nowadays, you can still put down 3 percent or 5 percent on a home to buy it and then flip it, or to let it appreciate and sell it in the future and make additional revenue by leasing it, or there are a lot of different techniques where you can do owner financing. Owner financing is when the seller can't sell a home, maybe it's a bad market, and they're willing to carry that note for you; so in essence, the seller becomes the bank and you're buying it directly from the seller. You then still have all the legal rights to that property, so you can rent it out, you can fix it up, you can sell it; you can do whatever you want, as long as the seller's paid in full when you sell that home.

Shannon:

When the seller's paid in full, how does that benefit them if they're the bank? How do they buy another house?

Woody:

There is only one of two reasons why a seller will finance, in my experience. First is that they have enough income on their own, but they're happy just to sell it because they want to get a higher interest rate. Right now, if you put your money in the bank, you're going to get maybe 1 or 1.5 percent. If they carry the note on that home for you, they can charge you 5, 7, even 10 percent, so they're making more money on their own money, so they become a bank.

The other reason is that sometimes in a bad market they just can't sell a home. Let's say they owe $200,000 on a home and the home's only worth $175,000, so they physically can't sell it unless they come up with the $25,000 difference; so they'll carry their loan for you, and then as the market changes and goes back up and the home's worth $250,000, you can then sell it and keep that extra $50,000 since you bought it for $200,000. Then they are happy because now they get their $200,000 out that they already owe their bank, and it becomes a little win-win.

Shannon:

When you're actually looking for homes in a down market situation where people are upside down in their homes, do you look at the location? Do you look at the future projections for businesses, neighborhoods, etc.?

Woody:

Absolutely. The number one thing that you hear people always talk about with real estate, the number one technique, is location, location, location. I've had friends who have literally bought corner lots and then they heard that Walmart was coming across the street. This happened to a friend of mind in California who bought the lot for

$150,000 and had the owner carry the note. Six months later Walmart announced that they were building across the street. His lot went from $150,000 to $500,000 literally overnight. He would be able to sell that and take that money. Now he can play in the commercial business on a little bit larger level.

Most investor works the same way. You make a little bit, you turn that money over. It's really called compounding interest where you take your principle and your interest and then you roll it over again into the next property. There's also a great tax benefit to that as well. You don't have to pay tax on that money as long as you're rolling it over in to a property of equal or higher value.

Shannon:
What do you think is the number one mistake that an individual makes when buying their first investment property?

Woody: The number one reason why people make mistakes on their first investment property is they don't have a mentor. They don't have someone to follow. They don't have someone that can show them the right thing to do. They just hear their buddies doing it, they go out and they buy a home, but they haven't done all the certification, they haven't verified that this property's not going to have termite issues or meth issues, or something else that could really hurt them. They think, "Oh, it's a good deal, I can buy that and make a ton of money." The benefit to real estate is there's tons of people and there's tons of organizations out there that have already done it a thousand times, so connect with them. Join an investment club, join a company that does education, and then they'll help you limit your potential risk.

Shannon:
How have your mentors in real estate investing helped you to navigate pitfalls?

Woody:
We don't know what we don't know, and every deal has a potential problem, and every deal tends to really have a problem. I'm in the middle of a transaction right now where the home had to be lifted. We knew that there were some cracks in the foundation, but we weren't sure; so before we actually took ownership and before we

actually even wrote the contract, we had an engineer come out. The only reason I did that is my mentor recommended, "You know what Woody, if you've got cracks in your foundation that are larger than average, hire an engineer. Spend the six, seven, eight hundred dollars. You'll save hundreds of thousands of dollars of potential losses for a small investment", so we did that and it ended up costing the seller $75,000 to raise that foundation. Had we bought that home not knowing that, we'd be out $75,000, so an $800 investment saved me $75,000.

Now, after the home was raised, we paid another $400 for an inspector to go out and verify absolutely everything. What he did is he pulled off all of the insulation in the basement and found another crack that we didn't know about, so now we're having another company come out and verify that crack because you can see daylight through the foundation. That's never good. You never want to see daylight in the foundation.

They're coming out to fix that. Once again, the seller will have to pay that and we won't.

Shannon:
How do you help other people learn more about real estate?

Woody:
Everybody has that friend who is in real estate. I'm that friend for my friends, and they will always ask me, "Woody what about this?" Or, "What about that transaction? What about that home you flipped?" What I like to do is just invite them to come along and take a look. There's times where I'll take five of my friends and show them a house that I'm doing, show them the pitfalls and mistakes, and where's the benefit to changing it.

This one home, there is about $100,000 in equity from us just buying it right. I believe that when it comes to real estate, you make your money when you buy it, not when you sell it, so you have to buy it right.

Shannon:
You are obviously passionate about real estate. What actually inspired you to get into the industry?

Woody:

I grew up with my folks in a different generation where my dad was the traditional father who would always work and my mother would stay home. In the 80's when the market crashed and we didn't have a lot of money, it was a challenge, and so my mom became a realtor. She would list homes, so when I was very young, I'd go with my mom when she would go list a home. I'd walk through these homes and they were, to a kid, like a jungle gym. They were just so fascinating, and I grew up being exposed to real estate. I met some of the investors who my mom was selling for and it changed my life forever.

If you list a home as a typical realtor, you'll make 3 percent. The investor can make 10 to 20 percent. They're just taking the greater risk. The realtor doesn't have any risk. They have some advertising costs, but that's not a huge risk. The investor who bought the home, fixed it up, put new paint/carpet in, now is making $50,000, $100,000, $150,000 on a transaction. That blew my mind, and that was the second I knew I wanted to be in real estate.

Shannon:

What are some of the creative ways that you use now, or what is your favorite way to find a property to acquire a fix and flip?

Woody:

For me the best way to find property is to know your area, so back to location, location, location. The home that I'm buying right now, the one that had the sunken basement, we've been trying for two years to get this home. We've talked to the seller, he wouldn't sell it to us. Then low and behold we found out that he passed away, and then we went to his heirs, which was his older sister. Well, she's eighty-four years old. She doesn't want to deal with this property. She lives out of state, but because I was driving around, just driving by this one house that I've always wanted to acquire, I saw a car there. I knew he lived out of state. It was an investment property for him, so when I saw a car there, I just knocked on the door. And told them that because the home had been vacant for over three years, that's why it was neglected and the home sunk. Basically, I was able to get the home before it even went on the market.

Had they taken the time to invest in the property, to fix it up, and then to sell it, I would've been out of the loop. So to me the best technique is, take an area, a geographical area that you know well and trust, and then master it. Know every house. You can pull titles. You can find out when people are delinquent. You can ask them to buy the home before it goes into foreclosure. There are so many techniques to save yourself time because it's trying to find that jewel in the rough. It's always hard to find, but when you find one, you can pull out fifty to a hundred grand.

Shannon:
How do you decide if you are going to fix and flip a home or buy and hold it for rental income?

Woody:
If I'm in a financial position where I can hold it and I can keep it long-term and I believe a certain area geographically is going to go up in value, then I will hold it. I have done holds in the past, but on the fix and flips, those are the ones that give you large pops. Wealthy people, I believe, get wealthy by the large pops–fifty grand, a hundred grand, two hundred and fifty grand pops. I've made $200,000 on a house in thirty days. I can't save that much money myself, I can't save my way to wealth, and I don't believe most people can. You look at CEOs who have large stock options and a buyout takes place; they get a large pop of millions of dollars, so to create massive wealth, you've got to have large pops.

Well, as soon as you've had enough large pops where you've got a good nest egg, now you can afford to buy one, hold it, and if a renter does not pay, you can afford to make that monthly payment. I don't believe in being house poor. If you own a bunch of properties but you can't fix up the yard or you can't take a vacation, I call that being house poor. You may have a million dollars in real estate, but you can't afford to take a vacation, then you don't have the life that real estate's designed to give you.

Shannon:
I'd like to go back to when you said you saw the car and you just knocked on the door. Tell me how that conversation went?

Woody:
It's very simple. You can tell when somebody is stressed. You can see it on their face. This woman looked bewildered. This is the first time she had seen this home after her brother passed. She didn't want that

property. She lives two thousand miles away. She wants nothing to do with this property. I asked her, "You know what, I've been watching this home for two years. Are you the new owner? She said, "Yeah, my brother passed, and now I have inherited this home." I said, "Well, what is your intention? Do you want to sell the home, or do you want to keep it and rent it out? What would you like to do?" "Oh my gosh, I just want to sell this home," she replied, so I gave her an offer on the spot. She turned it down. I waited about a month. I kept checking on the home. I saw them doing yard work trying to fix it up. I went back to her, I said, "You know what, are you by chance interested in selling the home yet?" At that point, she was, because she just realized how much work it was going to be to fix it up.

You have to understand that if someone is going to sell you a house at a discount than what it should be going for, that means there's inherently something wrong with the home. Either it needs new carpet, or they had pets in there, or it smells. It's been neglected. Things are broken. So when you're looking for a fix and flip, they're never in perfect condition, otherwise they'd get top of the retail value. People who have these homes don't want them because they know how much it's going to cost to fix it, and that was the case with her, so it was really easy to buy it from her, to take that pressure and stress off of her.

Shannon:
Do you think that you can have real estate success being a one- man-show, or do you think that most people need to have a team?

Woody:
When I say I'm a one-man show I don't want to imply that I don't have a team and I don't work with other people because that's not true. I don't have employees that I pay that help me run my company, but I have a network of people that I work with. In real estate you cannot be successful without a network of people. It's impossible. You need to know a title guy, a realtor. You need to know an appraiser. There are so many moving parts in real estate, you need to have a group of people you work with.

When it comes to education, I go back to that saying, "We don't know what we don't know." Create an environment and a network, facilitate a mastermind, put people who are in real estate in the same room and you will expedite your knowledge. You'll expedite your learning curves. It is crucial that you spend time with a team of people who have your best interest in mind to make you successful.

Shannon:
What is your favorite investment strategy when the market is good and homes are selling quickly?

Woody:
In California in 2005 when the market was just exploding and homes were appreciating at 30 percent a year, if you bought a home for $400,000, in a year it was going for a $520,000, so in that market we were buying homes that weren't even built yet. When a new subdivision was under construction we would put down $5,000. Homes would take six months to nine months to build. By the time we bought that home and moved into it, we already had $60,000 to $80,000 of appreciation; so in an up market my favorite thing to do is speculation. Know an area, know where the parks and schools are being built, buy homes that are under construction so that you can flip them as soon as you close on them.

Shannon:
When you look at everything that you do in your life, your real estate investing career, your entrepreneurial adventures, and your life married with children, what legacy do you want to leave?

Woody:
I want my children and the people that I have the opportunity to come in contact with to realize that they can change. Regardless of your past, regardless of where you started, you can change. I believe real estate is one of the greatest agents for change. It allows someone, even an uneducated person like myself, to learn something, to master something, and then to make a very good income with it.

My legacy is that I want people to realize they can do it. That's the bottom line, that they can have their own life, that they can change, that they can become who they want to become regardless of their background.

As my wife would say, "We are just borrowing it for a time before the next generation borrows it." Since we don't take anything with us, I would want my legacy to be the impact I have had on my relationships. There is no doubt my life has been better because of the lives of others. I would like to do the same for someone else.